A Country That Works

Getting America Back on Track

Andy Stern

FREE PRESS
New York   London   Toronto   Sydney

FREE PRESS
A Division of Simon & Schuster, Inc.
1230 Avenue of the Americas
New York, NY 10020

For information about special discounts for bulk purchases,
please contact Simon & Schuster Special Sales:
1-800-456-6798 or business@simonandschuster.com

Manufactured in the United States of America

1   3   5   7   9   10   8   6   4   2

Library of Congress Cataloging-in-Publication Data is available

ISBN-13: 978-0-7432-9767-7
ISBN-10:   0-7432-9767-9

To Matt and Cassie

Contents

CHAPTER ONE

A Country That Doesn't Work

Does it feel like our country isn't working as well as it should for you and your family? Does anyone understand the challenges facing us? When did our incomes start to stagnate? Why are most Americans working such long hours? When did our lives become so crazed?

Late one night while watching CNN, I noticed a network ad for "multiple simultaneous news streams right at your desk." I assumed that was meant as an enticement, but I wondered, Do I need multiple news streams? And the answer was, I don't think so.

That led me to ponder twenty-four-hour news channels, BlackBerries, podcasts, Web streaming, blogs, 24/7 news, e-mail alerts, cell phone calls, text messages—all available while I'm sitting at my desk or driving in my car, remarkably, almost anywhere in the world. I have become addicted to information and want to be plugged in all the time. Yet how much can the human brain continuously absorb?

Our world is fast and merciless. The constant flow of information, this world of nonstop stimuli, is not only physically and emotionally exhausting, it is transforming the quality of our lives. Life is getting faster and faster:

- The number of phone calls made in the world in 1983 are now made in less than a day.
- Estimates show that nearly 84 billion e-mails are sent every

1

day in 2006. This is double the volume of 2003, and more
than *8 times* the number for 2001!
- The entire world's manufacturing output is ten times higher
  than it was in 1950.

We live in a time of instant communication: instant messag-
ing, instant access, and instant replay. This warp-speed change
has consequences for all aspects of our lives, but particularly for
the fabric of our personal relationships. Like many people, I
like instant communications, but there are moments that we
don't want to take only an instant. Like the time spent with a
spouse, partner, or kids. Yet, more and more, people are losing
the ability to savor their lives. They're working so hard, putting
in longer and longer hours for less pay. In fact, Americans
work harder than anyone else in the industrialized world. The
average full-time worker spends forty-nine hours per week at
work and only two hours relaxing.

Something as simple as a conversation with one's spouse
becomes a luxury. Family members are like ships passing in the
night—or in the driveway. Parents lead transactional lives
where they trade off kids and errands in a "tag, you're it"
game: *You take the kids to soccer, I'll get the oil changed.*

Two-thirds of Americans who work forty hours per week
report being stressed, leading to inefficiency and absenteeism
costing America $300 billion a year. Meanwhile, we're making
less. Economists spend a lot of time measuring just how far real
wages are falling for the typical worker, and just how much the
cost of living is increasing. Consider these troubling findings:

- The median income for nonelderly households fell more
  than $2,572 from 2000 to 2004, a drop of 4.8 percent.
- The costs of medical care, housing, and food have seen
  double-digit increases from 2001 to 2005. Gasoline, fuel, and
  oil prices rose 43.7 percent over the same period.
- Families have had to take on tremendous amounts of debt in

order to keep up. As of September 2005, the total U.S. household debt stood at 121 percent of yearly disposable income.

We have national debates about these problems; we write op-eds and testify on Capitol Hill. The problems don't necessarily get fixed, but they are discussed. Meanwhile, these other costs—of time, leisure, relationships—are on everybody's mind but nobody's agenda.

How can you quantify the distance that develops between you and the people you love the most? How many stories have you heard about kids who throw their parents' Palm Pilots, Treos, or cell phones into the toilet or a bathtub full of water? Who's counting the number of months since you last sat down with your spouse or kids and *talked*—not about the logistics for tomorrow, but about *life*? It can't be quantified, but it's a high price to pay.

We share a basic human need to love, play, and relax in one another's company. But what we value as individuals has to be reinforced by what we value as a society. Those are the family values America needs to preserve, and it will not happen by accident, or by the workings of the market, or by fate.

THE NEW FACTS OF LIFE

America is a gift. For generation after generation, from every corner of the earth, people have come to America's shores expecting to work hard, hoping that their work would be valued and rewarded. And, more significant, Americans have expected that their children would be better off economically than their parents.

The American Dream has helped create an economy and a middle class that has been the envy of the world. And remarkably, despite the Civil War, World Wars I and II, innumerable natural disasters, recessions and depressions, the emergence of an industrial economy, massive changes in technology, and the leadership of forty-two very different presidents, the American Dream has been preserved. That has been the greatness of America.

But profound changes and new forces are now threatening the American Dream. We no longer live in our parents' or grandparents' economy. According to Charles Fishman, author of *The Wal-Mart Effect:* "In 2003, for the first time in modern U.S. history, the number of Americans working in retail (14.9 million) was greater than the number . . . working in factories (14.5 million)." Our country, joined by the rest of the world, is experiencing the most profound, the most transformative, the most significant economic revolution in world history.

This Is Not My Parents' or Grandparents' Economy

Over the course of history, the world has undergone three major economic revolutions. The first, the agricultural revolution, began when individuals stopped hunting and gathering for survival and established farms and communities. That economic transformation took nearly three thousand years.

The second revolution, the industrial revolution, occurred when people left their farms for factories, and their rural communities for urban ones. That transformation took three hundred years.

We are experiencing the third economic revolution now as America transforms itself from a mass-production and industrial economy to a knowledge, networked, service, and finance economy, and from a national to an international marketplace. This transformation may last a mere thirty years. This revolution is globalized, Googlized, televised, on our screens and in our faces 24/7. It is relentless, unyielding, and disorienting, and its full impact is only now beginning to be understood.

The problem with this revolution is that today's economy is

not working for most Americans. For too many of us, life is spent just trying to catch up, instead of striding forward. Workers may not have degrees in economics, but they are experts on the subject of their own lives. *The Washington Post* regularly asks Americans what they think of the economy. They have emphatically expressed for five years in a row (2001–2005) their anxiety over their deteriorating financial situation. A majority of the respondents say that the economy is either "not so good" or "poor." In a recent survey conducted by *Parade* magazine, eight out of ten Americans said they do not have much left to save after they have paid their bills. Seven out of ten middle-income Americans report living paycheck to paycheck some or all of the time. Discouragingly, parents are losing hope in the American Dream. Fully 52 percent of voters expect their children to be worse off financially than they are. Just one out of five voters expects the next generation to be better off than they are.

This is a question not just of Americans' perceptions but of their reality. Our credit-card debt is at an all-time high, and our savings rate is the lowest it has been in over seventy years.

- In the years from 2001 to 2004, productivity increased 11.7 percent, though median income grew only 1.6 percent.
- More women were predicted to file for bankruptcy in 2005 than will graduate from college.

The Days of "One Job for a Lifetime" Have Come and Gone

At one time, workers went into the job market expecting to find a job at a big company — GM, IBM, AT&T — or the local plant, mine, mill, or diner, and to remain working for the same employer until retirement. No more. By 2010, 25 percent of all jobs are expected to be contingent, meaning that the workers who hold those jobs will lack the rights of regular employees, or even any expectation of long-term employment. One recent study showed that baby boomers, on average, held 10.2 jobs from ages eighteen to thirty-eight.

Creative Destruction of Employers

Joseph Schumpeter, an influential, Austrian-born Harvard economist from the midtwentieth century, described the essential element of capitalism as the process of "creative destruction." From time to time, creative destruction revolutionizes the economic structure from within. An innovation comes along that changes the economic system and in the process destroys the old ways of doing things.

We live in such a time, and it is not just employees bouncing around among employers. Companies are undergoing a whirlwind of reconfiguration. They are created, merged, taken private, made global, joint-ventured, spun off, and forced out of business or out of the country in increasingly short time intervals.

The products Intel creates at the end of one year's business cycle were not even on the drawing board at the beginning of that year. In my lifetime, I have witnessed the transformation of a telephone monopoly—AT&T—into a vast set of competing telecommunications empires where conglomerates continually merge and reinvent themselves by adding wireless and broadband services, expanding customer bases, and bundling discounted services. Now, with content and delivery converging, mergers of entertainment and media technology are on the horizon.

According to the authors of *Creative Destruction*, Richard Foster and Sarah Kaplan, "If history is a guide, over the next quarter century *no more than a third* of today's major corporations will survive in an economically important way."

The bottom line: In the next two to three decades, two-thirds of our nation's major corporations will no longer play a major role in our economy. That is a lot of change. So, if you are counting on your employer to be around for your entire career, think again.

AMERICA'S NOT WORKING

These new facts of life are creating a country that doesn't work for most Americans. A number of trends are accelerating, which—for better or worse—are not going away and need to be addressed.

Income Inequality Is on the Rise

As Federal Reserve Chairman Alan Greenspan said before the Joint Economic Committee of Congress on June 9, 2005, "[inequality] . . . is not the type of thing which a democratic society, a capitalist democratic society can really accept without addressing . . . it threatens democratic capitalism." Who would have thought that Greenspan would become an economic class warrior?

Perhaps Greenspan was convinced by the data. After World War II, Americans grew wealthier together. From 1947 to 1979, the bottom 20 percent of family incomes doubled, and so did the top 20 percent. As the economy grew, everybody benefited. But this is no longer the case. The rich keep getting richer: between 1979 and 2003, the average member of the top 1 percent of wage earners saw his or her after-tax income increase by 129 percent. That translates to a raise of over $395,000 over those 25 years. But the bottom 20 percent is still stuck in 1979—their average income rose by only 4 percent, a paltry $600 over those 25 years. That is an unacceptable divide.

- If the minimum wage had increased at the same rate as CEOs' salaries since 1990, it would be $23.03 an hour, and

the average production worker would be earning an annual salary of $110,000.
- Median pay for the CEOs of the top hundred largest companies rose fully 25 percent to $17.9 million from 2004 to 2005. The typical American worker's pay increased only 3 percent.

In a recent column in *The New York Times,* Paul Krugman wrote that "rising inequality is driven by the giant income gains of a tiny elite, not the modest gains of college graduates." Even notable pro-business moderate and conservative columnists are shocked by what they see. The conservative economist Ben Stein recently wrote in *The New York Times*: "This is a country at war. For men who are already billionaires to look for more billions by firing hard-working middle-class employees or demanding they take a pay cut is not the kind of thing that unites a nation. I'm a devout capitalist, but this is just plain ugly." And, again, from Ben Stein:

> For centuries, the idea has held that the stockholders own the company . . . But what has happened is that—as in a corrupt, failed third-world state—the trustees in too many cases are captives of the CEO and his colleagues; they owe both their places on the board and their emoluments to the chief executive, and they exercise no meaningful restraint at all on managers. The directors are instead a sort of praetorian guard, protecting management from its real bosses, the stockholders, as management sucks the blood out of the company.
>
> I am by no means saying this is the standard or the usual way business is done in this country. Most managements are still honest and hard-working, I believe. But far too many are simply in the catbird seat to take what is not decently theirs from people who cannot afford to be taken.

Our country cannot sustain its social fabric, rich heritage, and social stability—and support the American Dream—if economic rewards flow only to executives and shareholders and not to American workers.

Guaranteed Pensions Are No More

Another dysfunction of our economy today is that employers are no longer funding pensions, and the employer-provided guaranteed pension system is dying. IBM, famous in years past for guaranteed retirement security as well as lifetime employment, has retracted its guarantees. GM, an innovator in defined-benefit pensions, has frozen pensions for its white-collar workers, and Sears, Aon, Hewlett-Packard, Motorola, and United Airlines have all ended their plans.

The public sector is now following suit. Michigan's and Alaska's newly hired employees are not eligible for their state's existing defined-benefit plan, and twenty states have introduced legislation to cut or freeze pension contributions, or replace defined-benefit with 401(k) self-managed direct-contribution plans.

More and more employers are instituting new rules whereby they make contributions to employee 401(k) accounts, but the amount of those contributions can be adjusted, or terminated, at any time. There is no guarantee of employer contribution to employee retirement income.

As recently as 1980, 84 percent of workers in large companies enjoyed guaranteed pension benefits. Today, Americans are working their way into a retirement crisis of unprecedented proportion. Financial advisers generally recommend that we'll need retirement income that's at least 70 percent of our pre-retirement income in order to live comfortably, with financial security. But most workers ages twenty-five to forty are on track to replace only 55 percent of their pre-retirement income. Two out of ten retirees today have no other source of retirement income than Social Security, and too many of them are struggling. Meanwhile, less than 29 percent of workers under thirty-four receive any retirement benefit *at all* from their employers. Consider these chilling facts:

- Five out of ten men and six out of ten women say they have little or no money left after paying bills to save for retirement.
- A little over half of all workers report that the total value of their savings and investments, excluding their primary home, is less than $25,000. Only 23 percent reported total savings over $100,000.

Those who need to save more aren't going to just be able to start doing so miraculously. In fact, most Americans are now laden with record debt. In 2005, the United States had a negative savings rate for the first time since the Great Depression. If families continue to file for bankruptcy at the rates they have been recently, then by 2010 nearly one in seven families with children will have done so.

Already we are seeing more and more Americans age sixty-five and older who must keep working. In 2006, there were 15 million more workers over age sixty-five in the workforce than there were ten years ago. That's a 40 percent increase: astonishing.

- According to the Congressional Budget Office, only half of baby boomers will accumulate enough wealth over their working lives to retire when they plan to and maintain a similar standard of living.
- According to surveys conducted by AARP, 57 percent of workers age fifty to seventy plan to work into their seventies; 23 percent plan to keep working into their eighties or "as long as they can."

The current talk in Washington about solving these problems focuses on creating opportunities for tax-sheltered savings, either by increasing access to 401(k)s and Individual Retirement

Accounts. The idea is to offer incentives to save more. But the hard truth is that those incentives have thus far produced the opposite effect, actually increasing debt. Americans cashed out $458 *billion* of home equity between 2001 and 2004, in large part because they needed the money to support their families. We own less of our homes than we did thirty years ago. It's no wonder that the number one New Year's resolution for Americans is not to lose weight or quit smoking—it is to get out of debt.

The old retirement formula—no monthly housing payments, combined with sizable pension payments and withdrawals from personal savings to supplement Social Security—is shot. I recently sat in a departure lounge with three pilots from United Airlines whose pensions were terminated and listened as they swapped stories with passengers of dreams of early retirement replaced by fears of lifelong employment. Do we really want our airplane pilots working into their old age?

The Health Care System Is Dying

One of the most pressing crises is health care. I first met Brooke Gurley at a Labor Day 2003 rally with presidential candidates. Brooke is a nurse and a single mother. I asked her how she managed to make the time to work as a volunteer on our health care campaign while also working her long shifts and raising her kids. She said she didn't have it as bad as many others, and told me this story:

> Last week I treated a woman in her forties. She grew up without health insurance which is probably why in the first place she developed Type 2 diabetes. But without insurance her illness went untreated and therefore unchecked until she lost the complete use of one of her eyes. She began treatment to stabilize her condition but without health insurance she could not keep paying for it.

The patient had returned to the hospital and was diagnosed with renal failure. Brooke thought this woman had only one or two years to live. Recently, she called to let me know the woman had died. She died because she was poor. In the richest country on earth, no one should die because he or she is poor.

The American employer-based health care system is the perfect storm: Costs are exploding, coverage is eroding, and quality is deteriorating. American workers don't need Washington policy makers to chart the consequences; they live them. Employers faced with increased costs are cutting benefits significantly. A total of 45 million Americans have no health insurance at all. Eight out of ten of those Americans are in a family with at least one working family member. Most Americans, excepting only the very wealthy, grasp the magnitude of the threat, that economic insecurity is only one major illness away.

- In the past twenty years, the number of families declaring bankruptcy because of a health emergency has gone up 2,000 percent.
- A recent study reported that half of personal bankruptcy cases were connected to medical bills.
- According to a recent McKinsey & Company study, by 2008 the average Fortune 500 company will be shelling out as much for health care as it takes in as profit.

Employers are laying off full-time workers and replacing them with part-time workers and outsourced contractors to evade health care responsibilities. Workers, even those who work for profitable employers, are being pushed onto taxpayer-funded state Medicaid plans or face increased copays and deductibles. Hospitals now face a new and growing trend of unpaid bills from *the insured*. Even nonprofit hospitals are resorting to unacceptable practices because they are under enormous financial pressure.

While trying to organize the workforce at a large urban hospital, a nonprofit with the legal responsibility to provide charity care in exchange for its tax-exempt status, Service Employees International Unions (SEIU's) researchers learned that the hospital was ruthlessly collecting bills from uninsured patients in Tony Soprano fashion. One retired patient had been trying to pay off his late wife's hospital bills, but over the years he came to owe more than the original charges in interest. His original obligation to the hospital of $18,740 had mushroomed with interest to a total bill of $55,000—forcing him to live his twilight years in poverty. Despite having worked his entire adult life, the patient had no health insurance. The hospital pursued him for payment for twenty years. As a result of an SEIU public relations campaign and the intervention of the state's attorney general, his debt was wiped out, as were the debts of many other patients similarly taken advantage of.

Survey research confirms that, across the board, workers and business owners alike describe health care costs as their top economic threat.

Employers are right to be concerned about the effect of health care costs on their competitiveness. In a global economy, American businesses are handicapped by shouldering the burden of America's broken health care system. It defies today's economics to expect American manufacturers, such as automakers, to compete for market share when the price of health care adds fifteen hundred dollars to the sticker price of a new car, while across the border in Canada and in other industrialized nations the cost of health care is not added directly to the product's price. The business community must admit the employer-based health care system simply isn't working; we need a universal health care system.

Employees and Employers
Are Getting Divorced

Americans do not need a marriage counselor to help them recognize the telltale signs of the breakup of their long-standing relationship with their employers. Loyalty and the old social contract are becoming passé. Increasing rates of self-employment and contingent, home-based, part-time, and contract work are all signs of the untying of the employment matrimonial knot. The shift in responsibilities for retirement income to the worker is the most glaring manifestation, but employers are also shedding responsibility for health insurance, training, employment security, and pay increases based on seniority. Workers now see job switching as the best way for them to learn new skills and get promotions and raises.

The pain of the divorce is felt most acutely by American workers, as they try to find their footing in a new economic world. Self-managed work lives—where we're so much more in charge of steering the course of our careers—are the aftermath of the divorce. So, where are the personal trainers to counsel and guide us through this new terrain? Some institution—the government, unions, employers—must take on this new role of safely charting a course for workers to manage their work lives. More on that later.

WHAT DOES A LABOR LEADER KNOW
ABOUT THE FUTURE?

I can only imagine what might be said about this book: *A labor union leader talking about the future . . . Isn't that an oxymoron? Aren't they all stuck in the past?*

I have spent thirty-three years of my life working in the most historically vital institution for American workers—the labor union movement. As president of the Service Employees International Union (SEIU), which represents janitors, providers of home health care and child care, security workers, and public-sector and hospital employees, I reluctantly led my union out of the AFL-CIO, the national federation of unions. SEIU made that decision because we believe all unions must change to do a better job of confronting the challenges facing American workers. Reform was the only way forward.

As the president of SEIU, it's my job to watch out for the threats that confront our members—and all American workers—and to find solutions to improve their lives. So I've studied the current failures of the American economy a good deal. I have also seen the remarkable power of the mobilization of people behind a cause to make significant change. I've been blessed along the way in my career to meet Angenita Tanner from Chicago, Illinois. Angenita earned a degree in early childhood education and became a family child care provider: "I watch over these kids like they're my babies so their parents can go to work knowing their kids are cared for, loved, and safe." Angenita and forty-nine thousand other child care providers toiled for ten years before they were able to form a union—their victory sparked a movement that has spread to ten states.

I witnessed the courage of Mirna Blanco, a janitor from Houston, Texas, who worked a four-hour shift five nights a week for one of America's largest cleaning contractors. Every night, she cleaned twenty-nine offices, two hallways, and numerous bathrooms—for $20.60. Mirna and her five thousand Houston co-workers decided to stand up for their families, and won union recognition in one of the largest private-sector victories in the history of the South.

Through their unions, Angenita, Mirna, and tens of thousands of other workers have found their voice, united their strength, and improved millions of lives. Unions rewrote the old rules of work by winning the eight-hour workday, minimum wage, Social Security, and Medicare. These successes helped to create the greatest middle class in the world and raised the standards of all American workers.

After the Great Depression, American society agreed on an unwritten social contract that "a rising tide," as President Kennedy said, "lifts all the boats"—and he wasn't talking just about luxury liners. Economic growth, increased productivity, and rising profits translated into improved living standards for most Americans. We prospered together. When the market wasn't working effectively, two primary forces intervened to help the market distribute gains relatively equally: the government and labor unions.

The federal government adjusted the economy to produce greater fairness, raising the floor for the poor, not the ceiling for the wealthy. By setting progressive tax policy, raising the minimum wage, and creating the Earned Income Tax Credit (EITC), the government helped to more evenly allocate the proceeds of the economy.

Unfortunately, government, as we have learned, can also promote unequal distribution. The policies of the Bush administration that are trying to phase out the estate tax, and that have provided dividend and capital gains' tax relief and added corporate loopholes have lowered individual tax rates disproportionately for the wealthy. That's accelerated the widening of the income gap. In fact, from 2003 to 2005, the only group to see their wages grow faster than inflation was the wealthiest 5 percent of Americans.

The trickle-down theory has been thoroughly discredited as our economy has poured so much money into the wealthiest 1 percent without any real income growth for most workers. According to a report by the Federal Reserve Bank, 10 percent of Americans owned nearly 70 percent of the nation's wealth in 2004. The largest block of that wealth—34 percent—was owned by only 1 percent of the population. What's more, that top 1 percent saw its share of the nation's wealth climb signifi-

cantly from 1989 to 2004, while the bottom 50 percent saw its
share diminish in the same period.

In the past, even when the government failed to function as a
positive force for distribution, unions were hard at work. Whatever your thoughts about unions, there is one undeniable fact—
they work. The union movement led the fight for the forty-hour
work week, child labor laws, unemployment, and workers'
compensation. Unions ensure that everyone's hard work is valued and rewarded, not just that of executives and shareholders.
Responsible unions can help equalize competition in markets by
ensuring that every competitor pays the same employment costs
for cleaning or security as they do for the costs of electricity or
tax rates. Then, competition is based not on who can pay their
workers the lowest wages, but on who can innovate, use technology, or manage more efficiently. In this way, unions act as a
private-sector force to set minimum wages and benefits among
all competitors, and they don't come with the inflexibility of
government laws and regulations. And, as a bonus, unions do
not require increases in taxes or new government bureaucracies.

According to the Bureau of Labor Statistics' June 2005 survey of employer costs, union workers earned an average of
$10.27 more per hour in total compensation than did nonunion
workers; that's $33.42 versus $23.15. The value of the benefits
that union workers receive is double the value for nonunion
workers: on average, $12.50 an hour in benefits compared with
$6.38 for nonunion workers. In the all-important area of health
care, 92 percent of union workers are covered by medical benefits, compared with 68 percent of nonunion workers.

The World Is Changing

But now the world is changing fast. The economy has changed,
business has changed, yet union leaders have mostly stayed

the same. As a result, the labor movement is paying the price—as are American workers. Since the founding of the AFL-CIO in 1955, union membership has declined from one out of three workers to one out of eight, and in the private sector to only one out of twelve.

Today, American workers need help. But it is not only unions that are clutching the past. Politicians, trapped in the twentieth century, are unable to break away from the ties that bind them and enact meaningful reforms. They fail to understand that Americans do not wake up pondering whether they are in a red or a blue state. They wake up wondering how they are going to roust their kids out of bed, get them downstairs, feed them, and get them off to school, and still get themselves to work on time. Laden with ever-increasing debt, they worry about whether they are going to earn enough money to pay their bills. They are concerned about what will happen to their savings if they contract a devastating illness. They wonder how they are going to care for their parents, who are, thankfully, living longer but are also in need of more time and attention.

Like many of our politicians, business leaders cannot find the courage to call for much-needed changes in our health care and retirement systems—changes that are also necessary for business to remain competitive in a global economy. They hope to escape the full weight of these problems in part by morphing their companies from distinctly American corporations into multinationals for which the United States is just another market, or by shifting responsibility and cost to their employees.

If I learned anything in my years as a labor leader it is that you can't drive into the future by looking in the rearview mirror. You either change and make history or stick to the status quo and become history. America is in desperate need of a bold, future-oriented vision, a thoughtful plan for a country that works. We need new ideas and a collaborative, nonpartisan approach.

There are solutions all around us; we just need the courage to accept that change accompanies the answers.

A VIEW FROM THE TOP

I've noticed a disturbing attitude, voiced in many elite quarters, that America's best days are over. In her *Wall Street Journal* column, under the heading "America is in trouble—and our elites are merely resigned," Peggy Noonan, former Reagan speechwriter, wrote:

> I think that a lot of people are carrying around in their heads, unarticulated and even in some cases unnoticed, a sense that the wheels are coming off the trolley and the trolley off the tracks. That in some deep and fundamental way things have broken down and can't be fixed, or won't be fixed any time soon. That our pollsters are preoccupied with "right track" and "wrong track" but missing the number of people who think the answer to "How are things going in America?" is "Off the tracks and hurtling forward, toward an unknown destination."

I know an attorney in a large law firm that represents almost every major Fortune 500 company who has sold all of his U.S. securities. He no longer sees America as a good investment. His change of heart stems from an unspoken fear that every dominant nation will see its decline and, for America, that day is on the horizon. Institutional investors, like public pension funds, that once shunned overseas investments as unsafe, are now diversifying their portfolios to include foreign funds because they are not sure that having all their money tied up in American companies is safe any longer.

I think these naysayers are dead wrong. This is not Rwanda. Or Bosnia. Or the last days of the Roman Empire. America is a country with enormous wealth, creativity, intellectual capacity, and entrepreneurial spirit. A recent review of the world's research universities shows that the United States is home to thirty-eight of the globe's fifty top institutions. We also have a workforce with determination, pragmatism, self-reliance, and a drive to work hard to succeed in today's global contest. After all, as I noted before, we're working harder than ever before. But America needs leadership and a plan to galvanize our enormous capabilities.

Conventional wisdom that (*fill in the blank*) the market, or trade, education, high-tech jobs, or wealth trickling down will be the answer to our economic woes has been proven wrong. Returning to the New Deal policies of the industrial mass-production era, now seventy years old, is unrealistic.

A friend of mine shared with me an old West Virginia proverb: "If you keep on going in the same direction, you're liable to get where you are headed—whether you want to get there or not." America needs a new route; yet, to date, our elected officials, and business and labor leaders have not developed twenty-first-century policies to ensure America's continued economic leadership.

TEAM USA

Worldwide forces are stimulating American workers and employers to undergo their own transformation. Yet, even as individuals assume greater control over their lives and seek more flexibility and choices, many old, large institutions are frozen in time.

America cannot confront the challenges we're facing with constituency groups operating in separate silos, or like-minded individuals failing to combine their voices. Our country's failure to break loose from conventional wisdom and embrace the future is the biggest threat we face.

In order to continue American prosperity, a new American dialogue and a new American economic plan are required. Business, labor, and policy makers must shed their cocoons and form a compact to create a new twenty-first-century American economic plan on the foundations of the twentieth-century successes: valuing and rewarding fairly everyone's work; establishing a strong middle class; promoting innovation and entrepreneurship; welcoming hardworking, tax-paying immigrants into our nation.

Over the course of my work life, I have learned a lot and helped bring about a lot of change. I have seen ordinary workers like Clara Vargas, an immigrant from Cuba making $6.40 as a cleaner at the University of Miami, join nine other university workers on a hunger strike that captured the attention of all of Miami—America's third poorest city—and stimulated a citywide discussion on making work pay.

I have been involved in joining the voices of many citizens and communities to make Wal-Mart a company that embraces a more responsible competitiveness, through a grassroots organization, Wal-Mart Watch, that has sparked a national conversation about employers' responsibility for their employees' health care and overall economic growth. I have seen long-competitive advocacy groups that had never worked together join efforts to form a new coalition, America Votes.

I have sat down with employers who were once my most ferocious adversaries and realigned our relationships so that both they and their workers could be more successful.

Over twelve years my union, SEIU, has conducted three bold change processes that fundamentally remodeled our mission, as well as our strategies and resource allocations.

In every case, change was sparked by the courage to try new approaches rather than default to familiar ways. I have seen firsthand how a vision for the future, leadership, a coalition committed to change, lively debate, and a detailed plan can bring positive change to fruition.

The global economy presents enormous challenges, but America has a vast reservoir of knowledge and the talents to conquer those challenges. Will the leadership come from immigrants marching on the streets for the American Dream? Or from bloggers and DJs fueling a youth movement, or from a new political party? Or will an existing party wake up to the truth and speak its convictions? Will the 2008 presidential candidates offer a new vision for America's future, or will traditional adversaries from business, labor, and government have the guts to come together to stake out a new course for America? Who is thinking about the future?

My purpose in writing this book is to help galvanize the forces for change.

We have to do it, and we have to do it *now*.

CHAPTER TWO

Globalization Is for Real

The magnitude of the changes bound for America struck me on my first visit to China. The fifteen-hour flight in September 2002 provided me time for reflection as I emerged from the most painful period of my life. I leaned my seat back and closed my eyes. My daughter, Cassie, was gone. She had died a few months earlier, at the age of thirteen, of complications resulting from spinal surgery. My marriage was ending. A few months earlier, I had received an invitation from Kent Wong, director of the Center for Labor Research and Education at UCLA, to visit China and meet with the All China Federation of Trade Unions (ACFTU). Despite my understanding that visiting China to meet the government-controlled labor federation was heresy within the American labor movement, I accepted the invitation.

In 1925, the Chinese Communist Party established the ACFTU as the only sanctioned union federation in China, and it currently claims 137 million "members." In China's planned economy, the federation functions primarily as the "transmission belt" between the party and Chinese workers, with the responsibility for assisting the workers in the evolving economy. The ACFTU, a creation of China's premarket economy, doesn't function in the same way as an American union and was not the independent voice for Chinese workers that anyone in the American labor movement ultimately wanted. As China rapidly modernized, Chinese workers experienced the harder edge of global capitalism and the ACFTU found itself trying to work with powerful, antiunion multinational corporations such as

Wal-Mart, when its only real experience was as a public-sector association.

The ACFTU was eager to conduct exchanges with unions from around the world to learn how to better respond to the forces of the Chinese "market" economy, which is its own unique brand of government-controlled capitalism. But American unions had a policy dating back to the Cold War of refusing to interact with "government dominated" unions and would not recognize the ACFTU or speak officially to its leaders. I found that policy counterproductive. Most Fortune 500 companies have been investing madly in China. Representatives of both American political parties have visited China. From around the world, professors, students, journalists, athletes, artists, musicians, tourists — and unions — travel to China in acknowledgment of its rapid emergence as a power player in all aspects of world affairs.

I hesitated about going on such a long trip only a few months after Cassie's death because I didn't want to leave my son, Matt, or to wander so far from the security of my family during that difficult time. But I welcomed the opportunity to gain a deeper understanding of the challenges presented by China's entry into the world market on American employment and business practices. My meeting would be the first of an American union president with the top leadership of the ACFTU since the visionary leader of the United Auto Workers, Doug Fraser.

In addition to myself and Kent Wong, our delegation that September included another SEIU representative, Luisa Blue, and two other union leaders, Paul Booth from the American Federation of State, County and Municipal Employees (AFSCME) and Tom Rankin from the California Labor Federation. I realized quickly upon my arrival in China that this trip would differ from my previous international labor travel; those trips combined uneventful, private dinners with the host country's union officials. But it was even more revealing to learn that, as important as the trip was for me, it was even more important for the Chinese.

After I landed at the Beijing airport, the head of the ACFTU International Department whisked me into the diplomatic lounge, where they served me tea. Still dressed in my green travel pants and ratty pullover sweater, I was not anyone's vision of a visiting "dignitary." I was apologetic about my appearance, as well as tired and jet-lagged.

I was driven to my hotel and asked to prepare for a meeting with the ACFTU's leadership. After a quick shower and change of clothes we were informed—to my shock—that we were going to be received in the Great Hall of the People, on the edge of Tiananmen Square. Our delegation pulled up to a large building, and with much ceremony we were guided into the splendor of the Great Hall's formal reception room and treated with the formality of visiting diplomats. As the highest-ranking union leader in the delegation, I was guided to a lavishly carved, formal chair opposite the president of the ACFTU leader, Wei Jianxing.

Mr. Wei was China's highest-ranking labor leader, assigned by the Communist Party. More important, he served as one of eight powerful members of the Politburo's Standing Committee, China's highest governing body. Mr. Wei wielded enormous power over all the affairs of China, and his importance surpassed that of any union leader I had previously met.

With great formality, Mr. Wei grandly welcomed our delegation with a short speech, and then he turned to me expectantly. With consternation, I understood that I was supposed to offer a greeting in response. Exhausted from the trip and unaccustomed to such formal protocol, I made some entirely unmemorable remarks about appreciating the invitation, hoping we would learn from each other, and wishing to begin ongoing communications. When I finished, Mr. Wei made a slight motion of his hand and, in what had obviously been prearranged, summoned the Chinese press corps.

Several dozen reporters and photographers appeared and

began taking notes, shooting pictures and video footage, and I later learned that our introductory remarks had been recorded, translated, and broadcast to the press room. For the Chinese, the photograph of an American labor leader's "historic" arrival was worth a thousand words, and those pictures would soon appear in the *China Daily News,* in Russia's *Tass,* and, back home, in *Business Week.* The media coverage ended any illusion of a quiet visit and guaranteed a backlash from my American labor-union colleagues.

I was stunned by China. Despite all I had read about the country, I realized I held outdated images of bicycles, Mao jackets, state-owned media, Eastern European communist-style drab buildings, and agents of repression. Instead, I discovered busy roadways, Western clothing, CNN, shimmering skyscrapers, few visible police or military on street corners, and an economic behemoth. America's primary economic competitor.

In Beijing, China's capital, cranes dotted the skyline everywhere you looked. In 2005, China used over half of all the cement produced in the world. The construction continues unabated. Beijing is now encircled by six highways, like Washington D.C.'s beltway; filling in each ring are row after row of apartments and new condominiums, retail centers, and leased office space.

The development in Beijing was stunning, but it was dwarfed by what our delegation saw on our next stop in China's financial capital, Shanghai, an even more modern city. We traveled into town on a modern expressway clogged with traffic, flanked by billboards advertising new mansions and planned communities, and I thought, Mao must be rolling over in his grave. I learned that the amount of square footage of space under construction in Shanghai that year was equal to all the square footage of Manhattan. Their new bullet train can cover a distance of twenty miles, at a speed of 287 miles per hour, in less than eight minutes. American corporate logos dotted the landscape and newly constructed gleaming buildings capped with lotus petals made a glorious skyline. Shanghai's metropolitan area was as modern as that of any other city in the world. The intense traffic reminded me of a crosstown jaunt in a Manhattan rush hour, and the smog was thicker than any I had experienced. Mao's Little Red Book had been retired from the newsstands and replaced by a Chinese-language edition of *Cosmopolitan* magazine with American actress Sarah Michelle Gellar on the cover dressed in a low-cut, provocative red dress. Getting a morning fix of Starbucks coffee, that day's edition of *USA Today,* or a scoop of Baskin-Robbins ice cream was not a problem.

I met globalization firsthand and was overcome by the realization of its magnitude.

Since that trip, I've returned to China five times, visiting schools, factories, construction sites, working women's associations, journalists, and academics. I've been told of increasing factory protests. I've read in official party papers about strikes in Shenzhen, a city of 10 million people in the southern part of the country near Hong Kong. I've learned about the development of a new Chinese legal system where lawyers can sue employers on behalf of aggrieved employees. I've continued my conversations with leaders of the ACFTU and have heard the frustrated voices of Chinese union officials trying to deal with foreign-owned enterprises. In 2005, I hosted the ACFTU's delegation to the United States and sensed their evolving thinking in regard to the significant challenges of a capitalist economy and the urgent need to reevaluate their role in representing Chinese workers. In 2004, I saw the first signs of that reevaluation when the ACFTU resorted to traditional American tactics of "blacklisting" foreign-owned enterprises that defied Chinese labor laws, including Wal-Mart, McDonald's, Dell, Samsung, and Kodak.

There is no question that worker unrest is on the rise in China. Newly assertive Chinese workers, many of them migrants, contend with unsafe working conditions, excessive overtime, and abuse by factory managers. Too often, particularly as state-owned enterprises are privatized, workers are not paid the wages and benefits owed them. When protests follow, Chinese authorities arrest the leaders, who can end up serving long prison sentences. A study by the Congressional Research Service reports that there has been an increase in the number of incidents of social unrest: In 2005, there were more than 87,000 incidents, an average of 238 per day, an increase of 72 percent over 2003.

As China modernizes and further integrates into the world economy, advocates of free trade tell us that we'll see meaningful steps toward democratization and away from labor and human-rights abuses. I certainly hope they are right, but I wonder what will happen if China's rulers succeed in bottling a potion that mixes market capitalism and political authoritarianism.

The resistance of multinational employers to work with China's union—even one as employer-oriented as the ACFTU—is anything but unique. Worldwide, workers share a frustration in their efforts to establish productive relationships with multinational corporations; those common experiences have stimulated discussions among national unions about the need for global unionism.

Despite my several trips to China, I continue to be awestruck by its dynamism. In a country where over 450 of the Fortune 500 corporations operate, the ACFTU'S willingness to transform itself to effectively counter the impact of globalization has far-reaching implications for workers everywhere. The scale, cost, and quality of Chinese production have raised serious questions as to how much basic production of goods will ever again be performed in America.

One thing was now incontrovertibly clear to me: China was for real.

A dictatorship building a planned market economy by making huge investments in its future has an unprecedented head of economic steam that is transforming the Chinese landscape and the world economy.

Some facts:

- In 1990, the area of Pudong, in east Shanghai, was open countryside. Today it's Shanghai's financial district and nearly the size of the city of Chicago.
- By 2010, 90 percent of all the scientists and engineers in the world will be from the Asia Pacific.
- In the mid-1990s, the vast majority of senior positions in foreign firms in China were filled by non-Chinese. Today, seven out of ten of those jobs are held by Chinese managers.
- This year, China is preparing to spend billions on 3G, or third-generation technology, to upgrade their wireless phone networks.

Many experts are tempted to compare China's advances of today with an earlier challenge to American economic supremacy. It would be a miscalculation to equate the challenges America faces with China today with the competition against Japan in the 1980s. Japan competed with the United States by emphasizing quality and efficiency at a time when America was producing shoddy products. America was able to reestablish a more balanced competition with Japan by "making quality job number one" and investing in new technologies and work processes that matched Japanese quality and efficiency.

Our fears about Japan's potential economic supremacy were abated by a strong American business response. The competition from China, with its low wages and increasingly educated workforce, presents a far more serious challenge.

"THE WORLD IS FLAT"

Author and *New York Times* columnist Thomas Friedman documented this most remarkable trend in his recent book *The World Is Flat: A Brief History of the Twenty-first Century.* He gave Americans an apt metaphor that helped us understand the mysteries of the changes we are experiencing and the foundation those transformations are laying for even more change in the future.

Friedman documents in staggering detail the twenty-first-century version of the flat-earth movement. Nearly 2 billion workers entered the global marketplace after the Berlin Wall fell and Deng Xiaoping opened his country up to foreign investment. The expanded consumer base and the new pool of workers joined by trade agreements, the Internet, and digitization aided in the creation of a global marketplace where information, capital, and goods move freely around the "flattening" world. The person who answers questions at the end of our phone lines, does the calculation of our taxes, reads X-rays, provides our food, and produces our favorite products is no longer working around the corner, but may be located in India, and before we know it, in China or any other corner of the earth.

Friedman identifies the most critical features of globe-flattening:

- In the late 1980s and early 1990s, affordable, user-friendly personal computers enabled individual users to send e-mail through Internet service providers.
- In 1995, Netscape introduced the browser to the personal computer, making it astonishingly easy for individuals to find information online.
- In the late 1990s, software companies developed common Web-based standards, which meant that it was possible for, as Friedman writes, "the vast network of underground plumbing" to effectively communicate with one another, easing the ever-increasing flow of information.
- In anticipating massive computer breakdowns with Y2K, Americans relied on India's cheap workforce to handle the mundane computer work required to prevent a national computer breakdown. Outsourcing was discovered on a grand scale.
- China's entrance into the World Trade Organization (WTO)

in 2001 guaranteed foreign companies the right to build
plants in China, which released a flood of off-shoring, not
just to China but to other countries as well.

- The ability to "Google" anything, anyone, at any time from
anywhere is an enormous globe-flattener as worldwide every
person can access the same massive amount of information.

The ability of employers to operate in any market has
reached the final stage of development, and I have witnessed all
phases in the three decades of my work life. In the 1970s, when
I entered the workforce, companies were fleeing the more reg-
ulated, unionized, high-wage North for the business-friendly,
low-wage, nonunion South. But the South was merely a
waystation. Changes in manufacturing, technology, trade pacts,
hard-to-resist poverty wages, and cheap land created a business
migration from the South of the United States to South of the
Border. Along the Mexican side of the border, new factories—
maquiladoras—with U.S. corporate logos proliferated. And
now those same firms are leaving their South of the Border
waystations for the South China Sea.

American manufacturers have access to a worldwide hiring
hall, with unprecedented numbers of available workers virtually
lined up at their doors, ready to work for low wages and paltry
benefits. And outsourcing is no longer primarily a blue-collar
issue. A recent study of over two hundred multinational corporations, conducted by the National Bureau of Economic
Research, found that 38 percent planned to "change substan-
tially" the worldwide distribution of their research and development work; translation—outsource from America.

These corporations are searching for bright minds and they
readily acknowledge that the United States does not hold a
monopoly on talent. In 2004, while America had a record number of Intel Science Fair participants (sixty-five-thousand),
China had 6 million.

India and China have motivated students, competitive high

schools, and college graduation rates that now exceed that of the United States: According to Microsoft chairman Bill Gates, China graduates twice as many students with engineering degrees as the United States does; and India boasted nearly 1 million more college graduates than the United States in 2001. The global forces that reshaped manufacturing are now on the verge of integrating an educated workforce scattered around the world, ready to work for lower wages.

American workers are anxious about their early experiences with this new global economy, and rightly so. The jobs being lost in this country often pay significantly more than the jobs being created; in fact, the jobs created pay about 14 percent less than the jobs lost. This is a trend that threatens the maintenance of our middle class and requires cutting-edge American economic thinking to secure our children's future.

In October 1957, Americans were shocked to discover that the Soviet Union had successfully launched the world's first satellite into space. *Sputnik* weighed only 183 pounds and orbited the earth in a mere ninety-eight minutes. Our country responded to the news with a patriotic effort to join the Soviets in space by launching *Explorer I* and creating the National Aeronautics and Space Administration (NASA). The 2008 Olympics in Beijing will be another *"Sputnik"* moment for Americans, when they see the striking evidence of China's economic might. Will America respond with a plan as quickly and effectively as we did to *Sputnik?* This will be the signature test for our generation, and a history-making moment for our children's future.

COMPANIES, NOT COUNTRIES, ARE MAKING THE RULES

National governments used to make the rules of their economies and the global economy. National policies were often protectionist: subsidies for farmers to maintain their livelihoods or to artisans to promote national cultural values; tax or other investment incentives to help national manufacturers thrive globally; or tariffs or regulations that stifle foreign employers' entry into their market. But in the new global economy, with capital and technological mobility, trade and investment agreements, and "just in time" logistical capability, multinational companies make the rules. As global corporations continue to prosper and expand into new markets, it is only logical to expect their influence on global economic decisions to grow as well.

Across the globe, we see the mounting pressure confronting countries—from multinational companies. Employers warn France that its extensive vacation policies make the country an unattractive market for investment. Germans are told that their strict procedures limiting worker layoffs are "old economy." In the Scandinavian countries, tax and social democratic benefits are seen as investment obstacles.

Again, let's consider some facts:

- Forty-eight of the largest one hundred economies in the world are corporations.
- Wal-Mart, the world's largest corporation, employs more workers than GM, Ford, GE, and IBM combined. Its annual sales, when compared to countries' GDP, rank Wal-Mart the thirty-first largest economy, with sales bigger than the GDP of 198 countries, including Ireland, Singapore, and Venezuela.

Corporations salute no flag but their own corporate logos and, some would say, worship no God but the almighty dollar or euro or yen or yuan or peso. Companies built on the foundation of American ingenuity, loyalty, and capital are now growing too big for their country.

I bet Jeffrey Immelt, CEO of General Electric, spends as much time thinking about his business operations around the world as he does thinking about those in his home market, if not more. The question is: Will GE always be a U.S. company?

I once heard Anne Mulcahy, the CEO of Xerox, explain that Fujitsu, Xerox's Japanese subsidiary, earns greater revenues than Xerox in the United States. Her expectation is that the next CEO of Xerox may very well be from Japan. Will we then consider Xerox an American company, or a Japanese company, or simply a nonnational, global company? Will former U.S. companies fight for America, our values and our citizens? Or will they put their profits before all else? Will our business leaders be available when we need their talent to forge a new path for our nation's continued economic success?

We have created global capital, global trade, global economic treaties, and a global economy, but we neglected to create any form of governance for this global economy that could establish minimum wages, prohibit child labor, protect resources, or create policies to reward work. Although there are elements of global government in organizations such as the United Nations, the World Trade Organization, and the International Labor Organization, a global government per se is a utopian fantasy. Therefore, countries and workers need to find new ways to round off the rough edges of globalization and to ensure national economic vitality and social cohesion.

My visit to a factory in Shenzhen, which used to be a small rural community and is now a bustling city of 10 million mostly migrant factory workers, was a moment of powerful realization about the dangers of the new global economy, and a wake-up call about the leadership role the United States should be playing.

In an effort to get a glimpse inside China's factory gates and talk to workers directly, an SEIU delegation posed as academics. In that guise, we toured a factory that made children's clothing destined for the racks in an American department store. The clothes were made primarily by girls and young women, ages fourteen to twenty-one, who ate their meals in the factory and lived in company dormitories. They worked on sewing machines that were old and absent safety features for twelve hours per day, six days per week, for approximately forty dollars per month. With hourly pay, after deducting for room and board, of a little over one dollar a day, it was no wonder that Chinese workers not only made the clothes but also hung them on hangers and attached the price tags, leaving a higher-paid employee in an American city little else to do except open the box and hang the clothes on a rack.

After our tour, we met the factory's "boss." I had seen so many American clothing and textile plants go overseas to sweatshops, and now I would be able to put a face on the enemy of American workers, and to confront firsthand this exploiter of Chinese workers. We marched into his office and were met by a friendly man in his midthirties who offered us tea. After visiting for several minutes, he told us his personal story.

His family had been in the clothing business for decades and recently had come to own several factories around Shanghai. He had left his family's business, and this was his first job working in a factory not owned by his family. After running the factory for some time, he had been asked by its owners if he wanted to purchase the business. He told us why he had said no. Then he made a surprising plea for help.

He explained that this clothing factory obtained its contracts through an online bidding process operated from Hong Kong. Intermediaries for end-users would post orders from retail companies around the world on the Internet, soliciting bids from clothing manufacturers. Factories would fiercely underbid one another for jobs, he explained, and the bids that won were so low that, in order to realize any profit, wages also had to be low. Unable to make enough money under this system, he said he wasn't willing to risk his personal savings to buy the factory.

In a moment I will never forget, the "enemy" of good American jobs, the ruthless businessman from China, turned to me and asked, verbatim, "Can't you do something to stop this race to the bottom?"

I thought I was meeting an evil master of the global economy, but instead *I* was being asked to do something to stop the race to the bottom. Who is responsible for stopping the unceasing downward pressure on product costs and social costs that are often inflicted on workers?

Not surprisingly, China's growth as an economic powerhouse comes with heavy tolls. My travels throughout China added to all that I already knew about the negative consequences economic growth can have on workers. Through the leaders of a Chinese nonprofit organization, we met workers in the intense, electronics-factory high-rise complex of Shenzhen. Hundreds of thousands of migrant workers, mostly children and teenagers, were being exploited by multinational corporations, using outdated equipment with no safety features. These workers were risking their personal safety on a daily basis. I met with workers who had suffered unnecessary, permanently disabling injuries and were struggling to survive. One was a pretty fourteen-year-old girl who sat hiding her hand in her pocket; she had been disfigured by the loss of her fingers on her third day at a factory and was now too ashamed to go home to her village. For me, she and her injured co-workers are a constant, painful reminder of the price of social irresponsibility.

I have spent my life fighting to make work pay for everyone, and personally I cannot accept, nor should our nation, that this downward spiral will continue. As the world's leading democracy and economic power, we need to accept the challenge of the Chinese factory boss, and stop this race to the bottom. Imagine your daughter, granddaughter, or niece, at fourteen years old, losing her fingers, and ask yourself if low prices and corporate profits trump decency in our own country or around the world.

CHAPTER THREE

Change Has Got to Come

As I've struggled with the impact of globalization on America's workers, I've found that it's not just politicians and business leaders who have failed to face up to the challenges, but labor leaders as well. Fairly radical change was required within SEIU in order to respond to the evolving economy. Before SEIU left the AFL-CIO, it underwent a series of substantial, and somewhat painful, changes that empowered the union to represent its members much more effectively. Ultimately, the reason why SEIU withdrew from the AFL-CIO was that, while SEIU confronted its future, the AFL-CIO refused.

Perhaps the fact that I took the extreme step of leading SEIU out of the AFL-CIO somehow suggests that I have given up on the American labor movement. The opposite is true. In fact, I believe that unions are as vital now as they have ever been, but I also believe they're overdue for substantial change. It's vital that they focus more on expanding their base of membership, become more democratic, improve relationships with individual members, and find ways to persuade business leaders to work in partnership with them. This may sound like wishing for the impossible, but we're doing it at SEIU.

Unions, particularly industrial unions, were created in reaction to the rough-and-tumble class-struggle world of the early part of the last century. In 1935, President Roosevelt saw the need to balance more evenly the competing forces of the emerging industrial economy, and through the establishment of the National Labor Relations Act (NLRA), he gave workers a stronger voice in dealing with their employers: unions. And, the system worked: Industrial unions became a brake on unbridled capitalism and helped distribute wealth more fairly. They became a market mechanism to reward work—not just for their members but for American society.

Unions helped create the American middle class. They bargained for employer-based health care and defined-benefit pensions and fought for the interests of all Americans. They helped create much of America's safety net. Not a bad run.

Henry Ford, a leading industrialist of his era, understood the correlation between the economic achievements of employees and employers. Ford's basic equation for America to flourish was, "One's own employees ought to be one's own best customers." He continued, "Paying high wages is behind the prosperity of this country."

It is nostalgic to imagine a wholesale transference of a seventy-year-old union model or Henry Ford's twentieth-century consumerism to a brand-new economy where employees are increasingly self-managing their work lives. Today, muscle work has given way to mind work. One out of four workers will be contingent employees or self-employed by 2010. Individuals want more flexibility in their jobs.

Once, free democratic unions were seen in contrast to the government-dominated unions of communist dictatorships, and were a battering ram to knock down the Iron Curtain. Lech Walesa and brave trade unionists helped win the Cold War, destroying all obstacles to market capitalism. Today, those who have the ability to exercise independent power—unionists, elected government officials in South America, organized workers in airliner and auto plants, people in the streets of France, human-rights advocates in China—are seen by many as impediments to the "natural" course of economic progress. But we must not lose sight of the fact that unions have essential economic responsibilities. At their essence, they are organized voices of people, the embodiment of democratic principles, and crucial elements of economic progress and fairness. The key is for unions to find a twenty-first-century role in the American economy, and that means real change right now. This was the lasting lesson I learned from years of trying to better address the needs of the members of SEIU.

Despite more than three decades in the labor movement, I feel inadequate in that I lack a compelling story of my union roots, particularly when I am around other labor leaders sharing stories about their union beginnings. As others recount their tales, I feel myself shrink in comparison. My peers have backgrounds that include long strikes or arrests, and memories of scant, meatless childhood meals because their parents were without jobs. Or dinner conversations in which union meetings and negotiations were regular topics of discussion.

I was born to white-collar, professional parents in a community where unions were rarely mentioned. I spent the summer after tenth grade studying in Spain. I went to an Ivy League college and never held a union job until I started work as a social service worker in 1972. These truths about my upbringing are not traditional ingredients of a union biography.

Like my father and grandfather, I was expected to become a lawyer. For a time after college, I sold newspapers on street corners in Massachusetts, gave tests to applicants for Census Bureau jobs, and served as a substitute teacher at Benjamin Franklin High School in Philadelphia. I eventually became a caseworker for the Commonwealth of Pennsylvania. But as I moved from job to job, I was certain these were merely stopovers on the road to law school. That is, until I got my first job working for a union. As I took on more responsibilities and challenges within the union, the union spirit overtook me and it was clear that being a lawyer was not for me.

Reflecting on my life, I realize that the seeds of my commitment to the dignity of work, and to organizations that give hope, voice, and strength to ordinary hardworking people, were planted in my upbringing. It was best represented in an ethical will I wrote as part of my religious training. I imagined a world of concentric and cross-influencing circles; at the core of the innermost circle was the individual, grounded by principled action and an ethical life. Each individual was then surrounded by concentric circles of family, community, and nation, each influencing the next. In my ethical will, I urged my friends and family to " . . . state what you believe in and reach for higher standards than you have already attained." Those principles guide my actions to this day and, more important, are the basis for a country that works.

My mother, a college graduate with honors, had, in the custom of the time, paused her career to raise her three sons. She was a superb mom: positive, friendly, and kind. My father was a lawyer for a number of local, family-owned businesses. Over dinner, he would offer glimpses into the lifestyles and family conflicts of our community's rich and famous. His lessons were always the same: Being rich doesn't mean being happy. Make your own life path, not the one your parents want you to take. Don't take what we have for granted.

One lesson he taught me and my brothers particularly sticks out. Every Saturday morning, neighborhood kids used to play basketball at our local high-school gymnasium. One bitterly cold morning, one of my brothers came home angry, seeking Dad's sympathy. With the temperature below freezing, my brother had arrived at the gym at 8:50 AM, ten minutes before it was scheduled to open. He knocked on the window to get the janitor's attention so he could go inside the warm gym. Acknowledging his presence, the janitor pointed at his watch and said the building opened at 9:00.

Returning home after playing ball, my brother told the story to our dad, furious about having to wait outside in the freezing cold. "Can you believe this guy?" he kept asking.

My father inhaled deeply and responded, "This man has very few things in his life that he's responsible for and one of them is to open the gym at nine o'clock. Maybe he's really conscientious about the rules or knows he will get in trouble if he breaks them. And it is possible that one of the few powers he has in his life is to open and shut that door for kids like you, who have all the privileges in the world. No matter the reason, try and see the world from his point of view, and give him some respect." How gratifying that all these years later I've become the president of the union that represents the largest number of janitors in the world.

My father had lost his father at the age of thirteen and worked to put himself through college by waiting tables in the dining hall. He always went out of his way to appreciate people's skills and responsibilities.

The story he repeated most often involved a test administered by the army at the time of his induction during WWII. The army was in desperate need of engineers, and thought Dad, as a recent college graduate, had potential. After the test was scored, the army officer called him over and said, "Mr. Stern, you scored very well on the general-aptitude part of the test, but I'm sorry to say it wouldn't be safe for anybody to walk across any bridge you ever built." So when repairmen came to the house, Dad would make jokes at his own expense. To the electrician, he'd jest, "Thank God you're here, because I'd probably be electrocuted if I tried to do that myself." And to the plumber: "If I had done that, the house would be flooded by now." Then he'd tell the army story as his way of communicating that he valued that everyone had a special skill that deserved respect.

The town of West Orange, where I grew up, is built on the side of a series of steep hills. West Orange was the familiar tale of two cities economically and ethnically divided—"The Valley" and "The Hill." It was a stark lesson about class divisions in a country we prefer to think is relatively class-free. I grew up on The Hill, which was mostly white-collar workers, some Jewish, some not. The Valley was overwhelmingly populated by Italian working-class families. My school, the Hazel Avenue Elementary School, enrolled kids from both areas, but I was one of only a handful of kids from The Hill. In retrospect, those early school years became an important experience, because otherwise I would have lived an economically segregated life.

In my elementary school, divisions by religion, job status, and wealth were not apparent. I was good friends with Artie Bozelli, played ball with the Pronesti brothers, and gave my first kiss to Francine Candeliere at a sixth-grade "spin the bottle" party. In seventh grade, several elementary schools fed into Roosevelt Junior High School. I hadn't anticipated the change, but it wasn't long before the students paired off based on their parents' economic status, religion, and ethnicity—made visible by the choice of leather jackets and iridescent shirts or button-down collars and loafers.

Although most of my friends were from The Valley, there now was pressure on them from upperclassmen and their families to stick together and sever their friendships with me. There was a similar, subtle pressure for me to find my "appropriate" peer group. It was a sad but instructive time. On one side were my grammar-school friends. They were working-class kids— sons and daughters of plumbers, auto repairmen, and landscapers—who assumed, in many cases correctly, that they were being looked down on by wealthier and elitist children of more-educated parents.

A summer job at a local swim club serving water and picking up trash reinforced the lessons of the economic divide. As a water boy, I earned the bulk of my salary in tips, which I learned increased if you were humble, polite, and available when needed, and invisible when not. If the swim club's patrons were obnoxious, demeaning, or racist, you smiled and ignored it. That brief summer job taught me an important lesson: For many people, your job defines you. Service workers at the beck and call of others are largely invisible and are expected to suffer indignities in silence. When employers try to tell me their workers are happy and don't want a union, I always think back to the lessons of those few months. Silence is more likely a sign of fear than of happiness.

While I was in junior high school, the country awakened from the slumbering time of the Eisenhower presidency. We knew America was facing important challenges, and John F. Kennedy's election as president was an American moment of hope and opportunity for change. Yet, at that age, politics played a far smaller role in my life than my emerging interest in girls and my preparation for the traditional manhood ceremony of the Jewish faith, the bar mitzvah.

My bar mitzvah at B'nai Jeshrun Temple in Newark was scheduled for Saturday, November 24, 1963. On my birthday, Thursday, November 22, I left for school in high spirits, knowing that my training was complete and a party awaited me after the service. History intervened. Tragedy forever indelibly marked the day when the school's public address system announced that President Kennedy had been shot in Dallas, Texas. America's dreams of hope, Camelot itself, had been shattered.

I can picture my family and friends and thousands of mourners in the packed synagogue, grieving and contemplating the future of our country. After Kennedy was assassinated, America plunged into a much harsher process of change. The temple where I had been bar mitzvah'd was located in one of the neighborhoods burned by Newark's July 1967 riots, in which twenty-six people died and thirteen hundred were injured. Those were turbulent times: Freedom riders were killed, as were Martin Luther King Jr. and Bobby Kennedy. The Vietnam War escalated. Students for a Democratic Society (SDS) and other leftist groups sprang up on campuses. Camelot's sudden end left me and my generation with the troubling and unsettling notion that our sheltered world had been torn open.

My introduction to organized protest was a more tame affair; it took place in the first semester after I entered the Wharton School at the University of Pennsylvania. Penn required its male students to wear ties to dinner, and students were served by student waiters wearing white gloves. The idea of being waited on by my peers made me squirm. I thought of my dad working to support himself through college by waiting tables and wondered what his experience had been. When some of the more politicized freshmen tore off their ties and demanded less-formal privileged meals, I was all too happy to join them.

I followed my tie-stripping debut with something a little more meaningful, taking part in an effort to halt a university plan to build a parking lot on open green space. By day, we used a food co-op I had helped establish to supply sustenance to student protesters, and at night, we took shifts squatting in tents on the construction site to prevent the workers from bulldozing the site or the police from cordoning off the area. I should have applied some of that energy to my studies: The university was happy to see me graduate in 1971 with the informal distinction of having attended the least number of classes in Penn's undergraduate history.

After my graduation, I traveled to Europe, wandered aimlessly around New England, and returned to Philadelphia for a stint of short-lived jobs. Later that year, when I received a permanent civil-service appointment as a caseworker assigned to the Vine District Welfare Office, I welcomed some stability. Rather than my last stop before law school, as I had expected it would be, my state job thankfully led to the start of my union career.

The story of my official entry into the union world is rather anticlimactic. Despite its accidental nature, it marked the moment when my lifelong passion for the labor movement was born. The union heritage of fighting for social and economic justice and being on the side of the powerless touched within me a deep-seated belief in equity and community that has never faded. Ten thousand white-collar workers employed in Pennsylvania's welfare and social service agencies were represented by a newly formed union—the Pennsylvania Social Service Union (PSSU). The PSSU Local 668 was a chartered affiliate of Service

Employees International Union (SEIU), though it rarely used the SEIU name.

This union of caseworkers seemed a far cry from my image of, and previous encounters with, unions. When I saw the notice on the Vine District bulletin board announcing a lunchtime PSSU meeting, I was as intrigued by the meeting as I was by the free pizza provided.

After listening to a report on the status of the contract negotiations from the shop steward, Al Achtert, most of the attendees drifted out. But at twenty-three years old, I could knock down a lot of pizza, so I stayed and just kept eating.

The last item on the agenda, of which I had no clue, was an election for assistant shop steward. The union's full-time staff representative and Al Achtert huddled together briefly. The staff representative came over and asked me my name and, after my reply, returned and whispered in Al's ear. Al stood up and, with great ceremony, announced that nominations for assistant shop steward for the Vine District were now open. Without asking for my approval, he nominated me, called immediately for the vote, and, within moments, declared my election unanimous. In less than ten seconds my most profound work-life decision had been made. I was the newly elected Vine District assistant shop steward for the PSSU.

Pennsylvania was a great state for learning about unions. It was the home of the mineworkers and steelworkers and the birthplace of the CIO. Wherever you went in Pennsylvania, workers made things. Steel mills, clothing factories, mines, and plants dotted the landscape. Many of those hardworking Pennsylvanians were first- or second-generation immigrants whose families came to America's shores in search of the Dream. As a state employee, I worked side by side with the children of blue-collar parents whose sons and daughters were the first in their families to graduate from college.

This was when I really fell in love with the union life. I went to every meeting, helped write and produce the chapter newsletter, and became a member of the countywide labor-management team. At night, I audited labor-law courses at Temple University and learned a little bit about being the lawyer I had realized by then I would never be.

Our union, only one year old, was in the middle of negotiations for a second contract with then Governor Milton Shapp. When the proposed contract between PSSU and the Commonwealth of Pennsylvania was presented for membership approval, I became part of an opposition movement to reject the contract as a "sellout." The circumstantial, dubious circumstances of the settlement—involving our union's lawyer finalizing the contract poolside at a political fund-raiser for the state's lieutenant governor—had mistakenly blinded us to the results.

In hindsight, it was a great settlement, with family health care, big raises, and new workplace protections, but our Philadelphia Chapter's leadership was not persuaded. Not waiting for the ratification vote to be held, we led a wildcat strike. That decision earned me and my now-lifelong union partners, Eileen Kirlin and Anna Burger, much notoriety and disdain from the statewide leaders who recommended that members accept the proposed agreement. We struck for three days—more on principle than to change the agreement—before we were convinced by the negotiators that the agreement was a fair one.

Early on, I began to suspect that the structure of the union provided the staff with disproportionate authority for decision making, as opposed to the more democratic empowerment of the members that I thought was in the true spirit of the labor movement. The union staff took note. My leadership role in the wildcat strike was not forgiven, and when I eagerly applied for a newly vacant staff position as full-time field representative for the Philadelphia Chapter, the state officers rejected my hiring. Only after the state officers realized that our Philadelphia Chapter leadership was behind me and would be unrelenting, with no intention of submitting another recommendation, was I brought on staff.

I quickly learned a lesson in just how resistant to change the union would be. Our Philadelphia Chapter's leaders were passionate proponents of replacing the full-time, appointed, executive director of the state union with a president elected by the rank-and-file. Although personally sympathetic to the change, as a member of the staff I was expected to keep my opinions to myself. I remained silent, but there was an erroneous presumption by the incumbent executive director and his supporters on the statewide Executive Board that I was the behind-the-scenes ringleader to replace them.

One day, without notice, I was summarily suspended from my staff job, pending formal termination. The Philadelphia Chapter's officers were similarly suspended from their elected offices. The leaders of PSSU charged us with fabricated accusations of promoting disaffiliation from SEIU and financial improprieties; the charges were later proven to be entirely false, and we were all reinstated. But the message was clear: promoting change wasn't welcomed.

Under the International Union constitution, the suspended officers were due their day in court. The statewide leaders hoped to stifle membership participation by inconveniently scheduling the hearing in Harrisburg, 110 miles from Philadelphia. But the two-hour car drive did not deter more than one hundred rank-and-file members from boarding buses, seizing control of the hearing, and virtually holding the International hearing officer hostage so the hearing could not commence. When he called the International Union to explain his dilemma, then-SEIU president George Hardy realized that this was not the calm purging of dissidents he had been promised by the local leaders and International staff, and wisely chose to reinstate all of the officers and cancel my suspension.

Ultimately, the constitution of the local union was amended to provide for a full-time, elected president. The following year, I decided to run for the job, and won with Jane Perkins, a staff member from the conservative, central part of Pennsylvania, as my elected partner. Our political marriage turned into personal romance, and we were married in 1983; for twenty years we raised a family together.

I took over a union divided by age, geography, culture, and philosophy. Although young by union standards, our local was already suffering from the problems of too many established unions, such as low participation and overly bureaucratic procedures, and leaders who couldn't focus on the big picture. All in all, a bad direction.

That's when I learned how possible change can be. I spent six years transforming our local SEIU affiliate into a more modern, innovative, and aggressive organization. To maximize membership, we reapplied my earliest union experience of providing food as an inducement, and took newly hired state employees out to lunch for orientation and union recruitment. As a union with members in every county, our members and leaders often felt isolated, so our statewide, simultaneous noontime press conferences on short staffing, or new objectionable state government directives, created unity, trust, and common purpose. Our statewide leadership trainings drew all the leadership into one place for the first time, and created a shared culture and the opportunity to meet high-ranking SEIU leaders, including SEIU's Eastern Regional Conference president, John Sweeney.

Eventually I expanded PSSU's reach into the private sector by organizing nonprofit agencies and institutions. I faced off against Governor Dick Thornburgh during the 1983 contract negotiations when he threatened steep cutbacks in health care and other job-security protections. Things heated up when Thornburgh threatened to prosecute our officers for conspiracy to commit acts of sabotage and violence, based on a strike manual written by a summer intern. In an unusual move, he ran radio ads against his own state workers in order to undermine our members' support by intimidating their leaders. His efforts backfired: We were able to turn his tactics against him, and rally our members for a good settlement.

I led and won and lost some of the longest strikes in public-sector history in Pennsylvania, and learned a lot the hard way. I learned one valuable lesson about the disgraceful pressures sometimes brought to bear against workers, especially private-sector workers, who simply want to select their own representative to work with management on behalf of their issues.

Workers in a nursing home, located outside of Harrisburg, called one of our union's organizers to talk about their problems at work. PSSU Local 668 had already decided to branch out into areas beyond social service agencies. The nursing home industry was outside our knowledge base, but we presumed it could not be that different from social service agencies—a fatal miscalculation.

We held a meeting at the nursing home and passed out authorization cards for prospective members to express their interest, and 60 percent of the nursing home workers signed up. *Piece of cake!* We filed the cards with the government agency responsible for union elections, the National Labor Relations Board (NLRB), and waited for the election certification, and our ensuing glorious victory.

Then everything changed. The owner of the nursing home hired professional consultants—union busters. First, the consultants met privately with the nursing home supervisors, who then held one-on-one meetings with the workers they supervised. Everyone who has felt their stomach churn when their supervisor makes a "suggestion" knows that behind the velvet glove of sweet talk can be a fistful of consequences. The message was unequivocal: Management told their workers that our union was an unacceptable outsider that would bring trouble to the nursing home, and they made their prophecy reality.

Employees who continued to support the new union had their shifts and wards inexplicably changed, a transparent retribution. A veil of terror fell over the workday, as the nurses' aides never knew who was a friend or a management informant. Workers distributed VOTE NO buttons to all the employees;

failure to wear one was noticed with disfavor by the management. Leaflets were handed out, and more one-on-one meetings were held with workers who supported the union. As election day approached, pressure built and those meetings were followed by mandatory all-staff meetings. By election day, the workers were drained of their union spirit. When the ballots were counted, only 3 percent of the workers had voted in favor of the union. The powerful had crushed the wishes of the powerless by employing tactics that undermine the very foundation of a democratic society.

In the 1980s, Pennsylvania's economy was changing as steel mills closed and industries were deregulated; yet the union leadership of the AFL-CIO seemed indifferent to the consequences on the workers. Pennsylvania was losing union members, but no one talked about organizing new members. The Pennsylvania State Chamber of Commerce was gaining political strength using sophisticated means while our primary strategies centered on mailing flyers. In 1980, I became president of SEIU's Political Council, which had forty-five thousand members and twenty-one locals in Pennsylvania, a part-time responsibility but one that offered me the opportunity to serve on the Pennsylvania AFL-CIO Executive Board. I was frustrated that many of the state's union leaders seemed to prefer the status quo over change. After attending several meetings of the Executive Board, I sheepishly began to ask other board members why Henry Block and Harry Boyer, two longtime leaders of the Pennsylvania AFL-CIO, hadn't retired. In whispered tones, I was told that they should retire for the good of Pennsylvania's workers, but cross them at your own peril.

I then talked privately with other leaders, who said that if I could persuade several major union leaders to come to a meeting to discuss change in the state AFL-CIO, they would come. So I assembled a meeting of the most powerful union leaders in the state. Once they realized they had the votes to replace the

AFL-CIO leadership, I was shunted aside as the leaders wheeled and dealed. I watched, amazed, as the discussion immediately devolved into the divvying up of officer positions, side deals, and promises, rather than a discussion of how to benefit workers.

Two years later, in 1983, John Sweeney, then national president of SEIU, called me to Washington with the job offer to be SEIU's organizing and field services director and I accepted.

I left Pennsylvania more fully appreciating the growing ramifications for workers whose leaders avoided asking hard questions about a changing world. The hopes and dreams of members came second to the status quo. Unions' early failure to respond to a changing economy led to the crisis that fractured the American labor movement two decades later.

But my time in Pennsylvania taught me two fundamental lessons: First, unions allow the powerless to unite their strength and become more powerful. This is an essential role in ensuring fairness for workers and should never be underestimated. Second, the ways in which unions were structured and doing business had to change.

There is no question that the failure of American labor laws to adequately protect workers' rights is a stain on our democracy. The National Labor Relations Act (NLRA), first enacted into law in 1935 as the Wagner Act, extended legal protection to private-sector workers who wanted to organize a union. The law set out the basic rules governing collective bargaining and the economic leverage available to workers and their employers. It also established the National Labor Relations Board (NLRB), an independent government agency to oversee the process for certifying a union's status as the workers' collective-bargaining representative and to judge alleged violations and order remedies if necessary.

The original construct was simple. If a majority of workers at a workplace signed cards to authorize a union to represent them, the employer was required to recognize the union and to begin bargaining in good faith to reach a contract. If just 30 percent of the workers signed the union authorization cards or petitioned for a union election, an election was scheduled immediately and the workers' decision about whether to form a union was generally final.

The promise of the NLRA, now over seventy years old, has been gutted by subsequent statutory amendments, NLRB and court decisions, and widespread company practices. Employers no longer have to recognize the union based on verification of signed authorization cards. Instead, the employer can insist that the question be submitted to a vote in an NLRB election.

While that might not seem a bad development, over the years the NLRB election procedure has become a frustrating process for workers and a litigation nightmare. Once workers have petitioned for an NLRB election, management lawyers counter with a long list of legal maneuvers that can stymie the workers' decision to elect a union from being honored for months, if not years. It is not uncommon for employers to seek to delay the election so that they have time to threaten or intimidate workers. Indirect threats are made, as well as blatant intimidation. Supervisors will hold private, one-on-one meetings with employees to let them know—through a wide array of subtle and not-so-subtle messages—that they should not vote for a union. Union supporters are not permitted access to workers during the election campaign. The NLRB remedies for unlawful firings are shockingly slow and ineffective. It's a one-sided debate under the employer's control.

Studies reveal that:

- Every twenty-three minutes, a worker is fired or discriminated against for his or her support of a union.
- Thirty percent of employers fire pro-union workers in an effort to undermine support for the union and remove union leaders from the workplace.
- Half of all employers (49 percent) threaten to close a work

site when workers try to form a union, but only 2 percent actually do so.

- Half of all employers (51 percent) coerce workers into opposing unions with bribery or favoritism.
- Eight out of ten employers (82 percent) hire high-priced union-busting consultants to fight union-organizing drives.
- Nine out of ten employers (91 percent) force employees to attend one-on-one anti-union meetings with their supervisors.

Because the company suffers no punitive damages, illegally firing workers has no real-world remedies, and an entire anti-union consulting industry has grown wealthy over comprehensive plans to frustrate unionization at any cost. Fewer workers use the formal National Labor Relations Board process to form a union because they want to avoid employer anti-union campaigns and drawn-out legal appeals.

And there is another major flaw in the system. One out of four workers in today's economy is completely shut out of the federal labor-law system, designed at the height of the industrial economy, so they don't benefit even from the minimal NLRA protections that apply to union organizing. These excluded workers include the thousands who are misclassified as independent contractors—many of whom hold jobs as homecare workers, child care workers, truck drivers, taxicab drivers, and computer technicians, to name a few—who are not covered by the law. Add to that number 11 million undocumented immigrant workers—many in low-wage jobs—who are denied any back-pay remedy if illegally fired for union organizing due to the 2002 U.S. Supreme Court decision in *Hoffman Plastics v. NLRB.* Adding to the law's exclusion are workers (such as charge nurses in hospitals and nursing homes) often improperly classified as NLRA supervisors.

As SEIU's new organizing director, I learned that many of the challenges facing unions today were of our own making, largely because organizing new workers into unions was underfunded and undervalued. Over time, union organizing became a low-prestige function, and eventually internal union politics created a perverse disincentive to pursuing a career as an organizer. Promotion, power, and glory came from being a tough bargainer and fighting for existing members who voted in union elections. Union-organizing jobs were largely viewed as career-ending choices, a place for political losers and the uninspired. While the job of organizing director for SEIU was a big step up for me, it wasn't a high-stature job within the union. On top of that, although SEIU was the seventh-largest union in the country at that time, it lacked a public profile, and was disparagingly referred to as "SEIwho?"

SEIU needed to change, and John Sweeney knew it. He wanted to modernize our union, and in 1984 he presented an ambitious, thoughtful plan that would: better equip our local organizations to negotiate effectively; increase the role of the national office to produce corporate research; coordinate approaches to common employers; and invest more resources in organizing new members. My assignment was to develop new strategies to expand the union's membership. That was a challenge I relished sinking my teeth into.

CHAPTER FOUR

A Story of Transformation

During the early 1980s, most national unions spent less than 5 percent of their budgets on growth. Unlike businesses that continually invest in increasing sales or market share, unions seemed oblivious to the relationship between their own resource allocation and their ability to grow stronger. This neglect was a self-inflicted wound that sapped union strength. Changes in the economy, the outsourcing of jobs, foreign imports, and new technologies deepened labor's wounds. The union movement watched as its membership in the automobile, steel, and textile industries fell. Most unions did not adjust adequately to these changes, and some buried their heads in the sand. Like Pangloss, the extreme optimist in Voltaire's *Candide*, they just hoped things would work out for the best.

Unions concentrated their energy on desperately trying to protect existing members in declining industries but disregarded employees in emerging ones. This neglect allowed newly created companies in the service, technology, and communications sectors to expand without unions—clearly a recipe for disaster. The sectors of the economy that were losing jobs had a much higher percentage of unionization than did the nonunion sectors of the economy that were growing, resulting in a decline in union density (the proportion of the workforce that is represented by unions). From the apex of union representation in the American workforce, when one out of every three workers was unionized, it slid to 19 percent in 1984.

For the next twelve years, with President Sweeney's support, we elevated the role of SEIU organizing and organizers. We recruited organizers from other unions. We broke tradition by hiring college graduates in addition to existing rank-and-file members. We promoted any SEIU organizer who showed potential. Without successful models in other unions to copy, we were forced to experiment. When we failed, we retooled and tried again.

Within eight years, SEIU nearly doubled in size, from under 600,000 to over 1 million members. Part of the growth was due to President Sweeney's leadership style and SEIU's collaborative approach with non–AFL-CIO unions. In a few years, over fifty independent public organizations affiliated with SEIU, dramatically increasing our public-sector membership and expanding our presence in California, Oregon, and Massachusetts.

But it was SEIU's industry campaigns for janitors, long-term caregivers, and public workers that expanded our profile as a union that stood up for low-wage workers. The Justice for Janitors campaign, the Dignity, Rights, and Respect campaign for nursing home workers, and the We're Worth It! effort for public-sector workers were like crusades.

Our signature effort, Justice for Janitors, sought to rebuild the founding core, the soul, of SEIU—janitors. That campaign taught me a great deal about the ways in which unions need to evolve. SEIU was founded at a time when skilled workers dominated the labor movement. The AFL had refused SEIU's admission several times on the grounds that its core members, janitors, "lacked a trade." Undeterred, SEIU continued to reapply until 1921, when it was given an AFL membership charter. Those early rejections ingrained in SEIU a culture that continues to this day: to stand up for workers considered invisible—often immigrants, always underpaid—workers other unions don't want to represent.

To reinvigorate our efforts to organize janitors, we began by researching the facts, and it was not a pretty picture. Stephen

Lerner, SEIU's building service organizing director, reported that in eighteen of our twenty-one janitors' unions, membership was in dramatic decline, work was being part-timed, and health insurance and wages were on a downward trajectory. A number of factors fueled the decline.

First, the industry was changing. Cleaning was no longer provided by the building owners but was contracted out to cleaning companies, which were becoming larger and more sophisticated. These cleaning companies were gaining market share, yet they had no allegiance to long-standing local union relationships.

Second, employers were hiring Latino immigrants, and our white and African-American union leaders could neither communicate with nor relate to the new, largely Hispanic workforce.

Third, our local leaders preferred to expand efforts in the public and health care sectors where turnover was lower, wages were higher, and workplaces were larger than in the janitorial field. Those efforts were more likely to result in a larger, more stable resource base for the union. Finally, employers resisted their janitors' efforts at unionization, particularly when union wages and benefits made them less competitive.

Our new organizing tactics were a little more sophisticated—not to mention legal—than ones from what some considered the "good old days" of the 1930s and 1940s. Legend has it that organizers used BB guns to shoot out the windows of office buildings of recalcitrant employers, flushed down toilets specially mixed chemicals that clogged pipes and ruined plumbing systems, or threw stink bombs into office-building lobbies and elevators.

When we met the union cleaning contractors who employed the janitors, they complained bitterly to Stephen and me: *You guys can't protect the wage.* This was their way of saying that they were losing existing accounts and bids for new work to nonunion competitors. They were at a disadvantage when they had to pay the union contract's wages and benefits while nonunion employers were free to operate while offering only the minimum wage and meager benefits.

This was my first real lesson in competitive business economics and it was seared into my brain. Employers live in a competitive world. Management sees its primary obligation as making the company financially successful to its shareholders. I realized that our priority should not be to make unionized employers noncompetitive by raising the wages and benefits they offered their employees over the nonunion company's wages in the market. Instead, our priority should be to *contribute* to our employers' success by organizing *all* their competitors. Only then would we be able to bargain contracts that set the same minimum standards for all the competing employers and thus take wage differentials off the table.

If wages are like electricity—where every employer pays the same rates—then efficiency, innovation, and quality will drive success. Employers may complain about the price of labor, but at least they are reassured that their competitors don't have an advantage over them.

In high-turnover, low-skill industries, unions are the only brake on the race to the bottom other than the minimum wage, and the only force to raise the floor. Learning to appreciate employers' competitive reality and attempting to create or add value to their business models became a basic operating principle of SEIU's strategies. It was simple: Either we brought up the wages and benefits of all the workers in the market, or the nonunion workers' wages and benefits were going to drag down the standards of all the workers.

We thought the theory was brilliant, a win-win situation. But practically speaking, finding employers to meet us halfway or even part of the way was nearly impossible. Changing nonunion employers' attitudes was, and remains, a monumental challenge. They often don't believe that partnerships with unions are possible, nor are they able to overcome their prejudices against unions in order to establish a different kind of relationship with a union that could add value to their bottom line.

We realized that our biggest strategic challenges came down to two basic questions: First, how could we build relationships with employers that added value to their businesses as well as to our workers' paychecks? Second, with labor laws so archaic, how could we find ways for workers to make free and fair choices about union representation without shedding blood at their workplaces? The former required the power of persuasion, and the latter the persuasion of power.

Although we preferred to lead with the power of persuasion, with many resistant employers we were often left no choice but to use the persuasion of power. In those cases, we issued reports that documented the disparity between the lives of the workers and the CEOs who managed the companies where they worked. We publicized company failures to meet product- or worker-safety regulations. We talked with members of the companies' boards of directors. We submitted shareholders' resolutions and mobilized community supporters. We asked elected leaders to intervene. And, of course, we also used effective old-school tactics: We demonstrated, picketed, and led strikes when necessary.

Our campaign to organize janitors of contractors who cleaned Apple Computer's facility in Silicon Valley was one of our early successes in taking our campaign to the public. With Apple, we held pickets and hunger strikes and took out a full-page ad in *The New York Times* to publicize workplace irregularities and charges of sexual harassment against the contractor. Once we enlisted the support of Apple's European pension-fund investors, Apple decided to take responsibility for the contracted janitors, and after signing up a majority of the workers we were able to begin negotiations. Now Silicon Valley's local SEIU chapter is working with the industry to obtain computers for the janitors and their children, in a more forward-looking relationship.

Creativity, publicity, and morality were the name of the game. In Denver, one of our staff members, dressed as Santa Claus, was arrested in the lobby of a major corporate headquarters while highlighting the disappointment of the workers' children when they would not receive any Christmas presents due to their parents' inadequate pay.

In the early 1990s, our SEIU janitors' "baseball team" traveled in buses to visit Mortimer Zuckerman at his annual celebrity softball game in Sag Harbor, New York. He was chair of the board of Boston Properties, a major real-estate developer, and editor-in-chief of *U.S. News & World Report,* yet we could not get his company's managers to treat equitably the janitors who cleaned their buildings in Washington, D.C. In an attempt at humor, we printed baseball cards with Zuckerman's picture on the front, nicknaming him—"Trash Can." On the bio on the back of the baseball card, we wrote, "Justice for Janitors scouts consider Mort "Trash Can" Zuckerman a top prospect for major league decency and fair play. . . . [T]his multimillionaire is smart . . . good athlete, and all-around player—he's built a personal fortune estimated at $350 million as a commercial real estate developer and publisher. . . . The word is that Justice for Janitors wants to sign Mort for their Washington D.C. team . . ." The janitors passed out the cards at the game; Zuckerman tried to pretend that we didn't exist, but years after the campaign we developed an ongoing relationship with his company, Boston Properties.

When other avenues of resolution failed, we took our campaign to a more dramatic level, using acts of civil disobedience such as blocking bridges and streets across the country, including the Fourteenth Street Bridge in Washington, D.C. Janitors and their supporters sat peacefully in intersections, halting traffic, and waited to be arrested, hoping camera crews would arrive in time. These were moral statements with personal consequences, and we got results.

Despite our best efforts, our civil disobedience activities did not always remain nonviolent. In 1990, a peaceful Justice for Janitors demonstration in Century City turned into a police riot. Officers with shields and billy clubs attacked the demonstrators—clergy were bleeding and protesters were hospitalized, including a pregnant woman who miscarried. The city was outraged. As the public learned of the events of that day, the tide turned and even more religious, community, and elected leaders joined the struggle, and the cry of "Sí, Se Puede"—Yes We Can—reverberated throughout the city of Los Angeles until janitors finally achieved justice.

But while SEIU was stirring up the streets, gaining new strength, and finding new pathways to success, over at the AFL-CIO a storm was brewing. After the disastrous 1994 congressional elections when Democrats lost both houses of Congress, a movement for change surfaced within the AFL-CIO. The incumbent president, Lane Kirkland, then seventy-two, seemed indifferent to the growing decline of union membership and its decreasing political power. His complacent response that the pendulum would swing back toward unions was not reassuring. The dissident union presidents of major affiliates of the AFL-CIO recognized that there were multiple problems at the root of the ailing labor movement's dilemma, but most thought a change in leadership would be enough to solve labor's problems.

An insurgent group demanded change, and when President Kirkland refused to step down, the dissidents chose one of their own, John Sweeney, to be their candidate to challenge Kirkland. Facing the reality of certain defeat, Kirkland announced that he would not be a candidate, and John won the office in a contested election with his mentor, SEIU's former secretary-treasurer and Lane Kirkland's number two, Tom Donahue.

With John's election as president of the AFL-CIO came the question of who would lead SEIU. John tried to finesse his longtime colleague Secretary-Treasurer Dick Cordtz into the pending vacancy on an interim basis until the union's convention four months later, at which time Cordtz could be elected to a full, four-year term. To the dismay of many within SEIU, Cordtz, once elected interim president, immediately started undoing the reforms that had made SEIU so effective.

I was now at a personal crossroads. I could continue on as organizing director and try to help SEIU move in the direction I thought was best. I could support others who were considering running. I could "wait my turn" and try to succeed President Dick Cordtz when he decided to retire; I could resign my position, and leave SEIU. Or I could risk my career by running for president. John wanted an orderly and stable transition and asked me to throw my support to newly appointed President Dick Cordtz. Like other senior staff, I was concerned that Cordtz would take SEIU in the wrong direction as he was already doing. I had witnessed SEIU produce such impressive results for members during those past eight years and I thought I could build on that momentum. I decided to run for president.

When rumors of my candidacy surfaced, and I still had not pledged my allegiance to Cordtz, he fired me. It was a clear signal to staff and union leaders that there was a heavy price for disloyalty, and to convince others that I would not return, he sealed my office shut with yellow police tape.

I shared with my kids that I had lost my job. We told them I would not work at SEIU for a time, but I would try to win election to Mr. Sweeney's old job as president. Matt, a normally carefree child not usually focused on my work, was scared. "Daddy," he said, "are we going to have to sell the house?" I confidently reassured him and Cassie that we would not, but in my heart I knew that a defeated, dissident candidacy was not a résumé builder.

I publicly announced my intention to become SEIU's president in February 1996 and took to the road, campaigning across the United States and Canada. Continuing in his efforts to avert a contest that was dividing SEIU into opposing camps, Sweeney, on the morning of his first AFL-CIO Executive

Council Meeting as president, tried one last-ditch effort to persuade me not to run. His proposal would have allowed Dick to stay for only two of the term's four years. With some regret, I rejected for the final time the wishes of a man I admired and respected because, in my heart, I believed it was wrong for our members, the union, and me. My campaign built momentum across the country, and when it became clear that I had more than enough votes to win, Dick Cordtz withdrew his candidacy.

The convention opened its seventy-fifth anniversary on April 21 in Chicago, Illinois, in the same Sheraton Hotel to which we would return for the fateful 2005 AFL-CIO Convention. But this meeting was a celebration of hope as we adopted a plan to change our union and I became the ninth and youngest president in its history.

On my first day in my new office, I looked out the window at 1313 L Street and reflected on how hard it is for institutions in Washington to keep sight of those they exist to serve. I thought about the janitor who works in the building across the street, cleaning its offices and bathrooms. He has no idea who we are, but every two weeks he sends a small part of his hard-earned paycheck to our union, hoping that we will improve his life. Our job is to wake up every morning and find ways to make his life, not ours, better. SEIU's mission is to live up to his trust.

RETOOLING SEIU

It was clear that our first task was to fulfill the promise of my campaign: to focus our national headquarters on organizing strategically for growth. Determined to follow through on our convention mandates for change, we began by shifting 35 percent of the SEIU budget to organizing nonunion workers and asked our local unions to follow suit by allocating 20 percent of their budgets. We declared a goal of becoming the first major national union to devote a majority of our dues income to growth. We hired more organizers and made plans to target growth in our existing industry sectors. To support this work, we began an education process with local union leaders and their staff to help them understand the benefits of gaining new members. Our theory was that increased strength in numbers translated into positive changes in the lives of existing members: strength on the job, strength at the bargaining table, and strength to hold politicians accountable to our members' agenda.

The 1996 SEIU convention mandates required a difficult and painful series of decisions: 144 staff members from the national office were given new assignments, many outside of Washington; six departments and twenty-one management positions were eliminated; unnecessary expenses were cut. A freeze on new hiring was implemented. Many of these decisions made by the new leadership team were not popular and were disruptive to staff.

Our decision to divert resources to organizing forced us to pare down important services to our local unions. We reduced our health and safety staff from twenty-one to two and dramatically limited popular research and educational services we had previously provided our affiliates.

On my first December holiday as president, I began to understand why many leaders hesitate to make hard decisions. To celebrate the holidays, I had invited everyone to an informal reception in my office. Staff, wearing black armbands, delivered their RSVPs and sang not very flattering Christmas carols about what they saw as my lack of holiday spirit.

Change is not a zero-sum game; there are winners and losers. Personally, it was difficult to put my colleagues on the headquarters' staff through so much anxiety, so quickly after my election, but reorienting SEIU was not about either my life or the staff's: It was about the lives of our members. I appreciated that a new leader has only one opportunity to make a first impression and I wanted my presidency's commitment to change to be irrefutable. Despite concerns from many quarters of the union, I steadfastly pressed on to other areas of promised reform.

Strategic Growth and Organizing

One of my top priorities was to structure our union to be more narrowly focused in the industries where we were strongest—health care, public sector, and building services. We did this in a number of ways.

First, we asked our members to do what many national union leaders considered unthinkable: restructure their local unions, some of which represented workers in a wide range of sectors. The plan urged each local union to develop the narrowest focus possible in *only one* of SEIU's major industries.

Second, in what may have been one of the only times in labor history that this was done, we asked our members in industries where we lacked experience or a strong membership base, such as laundry, hotel, and utility workers, if they wanted to vote to transfer to another national union that could better represent them. Uniting workers into unions where they could maximize rather than divide their strength was an essential principle of change. While some leaders and staff objected to letting members choose to transfer to another union, because it would mean fewer members for SEIU, I felt they would receive better representation elsewhere.

Several years earlier I had met with SEIU members who were gas utility workers at an inter-union gas conference. We had talked about how their industry was deregulating, their employers were merging, and SEIU was not prepared to give them the kind of representation they needed. If they had been health care workers or janitors I would have had a plan to help them, but because they were outside our area of expertise, I didn't. I still feel the sting of their anger and disappointment.

I recalled that conversation when I sat down again with

those members to share my conclusion that they should transfer to another union. Their first reaction was that I wanted to get rid of them. But as they heard more from the leaders of their proposed new union, the Utility Workers, about what they could do together, their excitement grew. By the end of 2004, over fifteen thousand members—primarily utility workers and laundry and hotel employees—voted to transfer to other unions and united their strength with the strength of other workers who did the same type of work.

Third, and perhaps most important, we gained significant numbers in both the public and health care sectors. Over the eight-year period from 1996 to 2004, more than twenty-five independent public-sector unions affiliated with SEIU, bringing 50,000 new members to the union in addition to the fifty independents and 150,000 members in the previous decade under President Sweeney's leadership. In addition, in a historic moment in 1998, SEIU merged with America's other major health care union—1199 New York—and gained 125,000 new members. We also gained two impressive union leaders—Dennis Rivera, its president, and Gerry Hudson, now an SEIU executive vice president. Just as there was an autoworkers' union, a steelworkers' union, and a mineworkers' union, there was now one major health care workers' union.

In 1999, we took another leap forward, further solidifying our dominance in the health care industry. Ten years of perseverance paid off: victory in the largest organizing election in modern labor history for 74,000 homecare workers in Los Angeles, California.

Homecare workers take care of senior citizens and people with disabilities who can remain living independently in their homes with outside assistance, avoiding the institutional care of nursing homes. Homecare workers—along with day laborers and child-care workers—are part of an invisible class who work in a netherland with two challenges—no employer and no union to handle their employment issues. No one wanted to take responsibility for the Los Angeles home care workers—not Los Angeles County, which oversaw the program; not the state of California, which paid them; not the clients who hired them. A California state-court ruling classified them as independent contractors, so legally no one was responsible for the workers of a several-hundred-million-dollar program.

Organizing a campaign of this magnitude requires tremendous commitment and staying power. I attended more local-union pancake breakfasts and cookouts to raise funds for our efforts in Los Angeles than I care to remember. The workers, as devoted to one another as sisters, had an unshakable commitment to forming a union; they saw it as their only hope for economic advancement. These minimum-wage earners paid union dues for ten years for the dream of having their own organization.

SEIU successfully lobbied the state legislature to create a public home care authority, like a public housing authority or a water and sewer authority, so that the home care workers had an official employer. Now the home care workers had an employer with whom they could negotiate for better wages and benefits—that is, *if they had a union to bargain for them.*

So a massive effort began to go house to house and neighborhood to neighborhood to find 74,000 workers who had no work site other than their clients' homes, and gain the signatures of 22,400 of them on cards, triggering an election.

Finally the day arrived for the vote that would determine whether a union could be formed. On the balmy afternoon of the ballot count, we gathered in a hotel ballroom in Los Angeles as the American Arbitration Association conducted the ballot certification. While we waited for the results, Senator Bill Bradley, who was then running for president, sat with the workers and listened to their life stories. He was clearly moved by the home care workers' kindness and love toward their elderly and disabled clients. After this meeting, Bradley went to one of his first presidential campaign large-donor events, attended by

about five hundred people; at that event, the senator coura-
geously spoke about the problems of low-wage workers—a
refreshingly different approach to economic issues that wealthy
Democratic donors don't often hear about from presidential
candidates.

When the count was finally in, we learned that we had won
with 89 percent of the vote. We marched on stage, crying and
hugging, for a moving press conference in which the workers
were joined by politicians and by their clients in wheelchairs.
Verdia Daniels, then president of SEIU Local 434B, the homecare workers' union, is a polite woman but she can shake the
rafters when she preaches the union gospel to the workforce of
mostly women and people of color. Her ear-to-ear smile that
afternoon said everything: Home care workers were invisible
no more.

This marked a critical transition from the days of history-
making victories for industrial-union workers in large industrial
plants, like General Motors, to a new era of service-worker victories in today's large and growing sector. The victory gained
national prominence on the front page of *The New York Times*
and sparked a firestorm of new home care efforts. With our new
slogan "Invisible No More" we spread the home care message
throughout California and across the border into Oregon, and
to Illinois, New York, Michigan, Washington, and Maine,
adding over 350,000 SEIU members. We were on the road to
transforming minimum-wage jobs into ones that paid suffi-
cient wages to raise a family.

From 1996 to 2004, my first two terms as SEIU's president,
the union had grown by more than 600,000 new members, a 27
percent increase. Our national union allocation to growth had
climbed to almost half of our budget (47 percent) and we had
over 450 organizers on staff. It was not just a U.S. phenomenon
of change. SEIU affiliated an independent union in Puerto
Rico and became the largest union on the island, and its leader,
Roberto Pagan, became our first vice president from Puerto

Rico; and our Canadian members, restructured, began new growth efforts and became greater participants in the leadership of SEIU.

Why Are We Fighting?

One of the first defining moments of my presidency occurred shortly after the 1996 SEIU Convention. The election glow had barely subsided when I dove into my first bargaining challenge as president of SEIU: I flew to Los Angeles to try to reach a settlement with Kaiser Permanente, our largest health care employer. SEIU members employed by Kaiser opposed its unilateral, cost-cutting, reengineering efforts, and a series of strikes had poisoned the relationship. After avoiding another strike and moving the L.A. negotiations back on track, I called Kaiser's CEO, David Lawrence. He has since told me that when he took my call he had no idea who I was. My message was simple—*we need to change our relationship*—and I am forever grateful that he took my call. Thankfully, Lawrence's reputation as an industry leader was well earned, and that conversation was the first of many that set in motion the creation of what has become the largest labor-management partnership in the history of the service sector.

This was a risky, colossal shift in approach. Kaiser employees were rightfully angry over a number of factors: unilateral decisions the company was making, their own ineffective strikes and concessionary bargaining, and their lack of involvement in quality of care. It wasn't always easy for union members to hear that their elected leader—someone who they thought should be fighting for them tooth and nail—was talking peaceably with the CEO of their company and promoting new relationships. Yet, members voted to adopt the partnership and grew to understand that although not perfect, it opened up far more productive opportunities. With Kaiser, we experimented with a new approach to collective bargaining that emphasized problem solving. Our members presented their concerns rather than make demands. Management shared their issues. Joint committees were formed to brainstorm solutions to our respective areas of interest. I attended an early negotiating session in which each issue committee reported on their progress. Listening to the workers and management speaking was an amazing experience: As hard as I tried, I could not distinguish the union representatives from the management representatives.

Our groundbreaking relationship improved the quality of patient care and enhanced revenue growth for Kaiser and produced some of the best contracts in the health care industry. It was a perfect win-win scenario.

Yet, not every union agrees with our approach. To this day, the California Nurses Association still criticizes SEIU's arrangement with Kaiser and has chosen not to join us in the process.

I successfully imported this problem-solving approach to another long-standing fight—the Justice for Janitors campaign in Washington, D.C. After ten years of increasingly aggressive actions, I decided that SEIU would unilaterally suspend our antagonistic efforts and negotiate with the owners a new way forward.

Today, we have formed alliances with hospitals and nursing-home owners along the West Coast. We have a national partnership agreement with the largest private homecare provider in the country. As we approach new relationships with public employers in the South and Southwest, we introduce what we call the "IQ" program—innovation and quality—eschewing traditional collective-bargaining issues and focusing on improving public services.

Like most traditional labor leaders, I had been trained to be distrustful of and antagonistic with "the boss," and I brought that attitude to the relationship. The distrust can be rightfully earned, but this class-struggle mentality was a vestige of an earlier, rough era of industrial unions, and our new service-sector union had adopted it without much strategic examination.

Today, I begin each employer relationship with an open mind and work to have it be constructive from the outset. There are times when a true "partnership" may be an unrealistic goal, but a working "relationship" that can add value to the business and help improve performance will result in workers sharing fairly in their employers' success. The shift in union attitude places a burden on employers to choose the avenue on which to proceed. We've still got a long, long way to go in spreading positive changes of this kind in union-employer relations, but there's no doubt we've made progress.

If the going gets rough with employers, SEIU is more than adept at holding its own and is viewed as a powerful force to defend workers' interests. We wage long-term campaigns that focus on the corporation's accountability to its workers and the communities in which it operates. We do so relying on great moral drama and high-visibility tactics if those are the only avenues available to improve workers' lives and to address the concerns of community allies. Even seemingly invincible Wal-Mart, the most profitable employer in the world, has had its image tarnished by Wal-Mart Watch, an SEIU-initiated effort to focus Americans on the impact of its low-wage, limited-benefits business model on its own employees but on all American workers as well.

Disappointingly, only a few employers have shifted from their "unions are the problem" mentality. Their lack of creativity and courage is an impediment to building a new model of labor-management relationships and to confronting the challenges of globalization. Asking our employers to make the choice of cooperation or confrontation is a dramatic paradigm shift. We have reinvented ourselves, but it takes two to tango.

The health care union 1199 New York, which had merged with SEIU in 1998, taught us a great deal about how to tango. Dennis Rivera, the president of 1199 New York, had created a paradigm-busting collaborative relationship with major hospitals in the New York metropolitan area. The political prowess of 1199 made them the champion of their employers' need for fair hospital-reimbursement rates.

The hospital industry's own efforts to increase its reimbursement rates were viewed as self-serving, just another interest group trying to feed at the trough of taxpayer dollars. But when SEIU 1199's nurse's aides, social workers, and nurses lobbied for increased state funding for the hospital, their more sympathetic faces reframed the discussion. While the hospitals were minimally politically active, SEIU 1199 was a political powerhouse, a fixture in Albany. SEIU 1199's record-setting political contributions and members, who could flood the legislative corridor when needed, gave them the clout to be the legislators' best friend or worst nightmare. Dennis and the industry leaders used their coordinated efforts in Albany to win billions of dollars of reimbursements for the hospitals, which translated into stable balance sheets for the employers and excellent wages and the gold standard of benefits for the hospital workers, including multimillion-dollar training and upgrading funds for the workers.

SEIU 1199's partnership approach further challenged many SEIU leaders' traditional "class struggle" attitudes about employers, but the increased hospital reimbursements being converted into improvements in their members' lives made other union leaders take notice.

SEIU confronted its image among our employers as an institution that created problems rather than solved them. Understanding the many issues confronting our employers—rising benefit costs, outsourcing, globalization, decreased public funding for their services, nonunion competitors with lower costs and more flexibility—gave us insights into how to enhance each individual employer's competitiveness.

Successes with Kaiser and the New York hospitals strengthened our reputation with employers, and we built on them with the ten thousand janitors who cleaned the office buildings in the cities and suburbs of northern New Jersey. In 2000, only a fraction of New Jersey's janitors were unionized, compared to nearly 100 percent in New York City. New Jersey janitors earned ten dollars *less* per hour than their counterparts across the river in Manhattan. The low wages created huge turnover and less productivity, and employers were no happier with the situation than the janitors were. For one company to offer better wages would have been tantamount to an army unilaterally disarming in the middle of a war: Cheaper competitors would immediately overrun its business. We brought all of the major employers to the table at one time, rather than one at a time, and were able to reach a settlement that raised wages and maintained competitiveness.

It took a lot of perspiration, inspiration, and mistakes, but we learned from each one, and became relevant to the industry. Justice for Janitors became the most successful private-sector organizing model in the last decade of the twentieth century because it recognized and responded to the competitive forces of our employers, allowing us to bargain contracts that greatly improved janitors' salaries and benefits and added value to our employers by reducing turnover.

Change Happens

I will never forget the day in 2003 when David Devereaux, who at the time was the COO of Beverly Enterprises, our archenemy nursing home operator, came to see me. SEIU and Beverly Enterprises had undergone twenty years of extraordinary, unceasing battle, which included long strikes all across the nation, Beverly's firing of workers who tried to organize unions, and its refusal to bargain once a union was established.

Once Devereaux and I were face-to-face, we acknowledged that our conflict had taken on a life of its own and we had lost sight of the reasons why we were fighting so viciously. We admitted that it wasn't working for either of us. Devereaux told me that the results of a financial analysis of the profitability of his union nursing homes compared to his nonunion homes surprised him. He discovered that when he took into account the lost opportunity to work on state reimbursements and quality initiatives, union nursing homes were no less profitable than nonunion nursing homes. We shook hands and promised to better align our interests, and we have. On a state-by-state basis we have worked to increase reimbursements and give workers more of a voice on the job.

The Purple Union

One area for internal change that had far greater significance than imaginable involved SEIU's identity—the decision that led SEIU to become "the purple union." When I became SEIU's president, it was less a national union than a council of local unions. SEIU local unions were using *no fewer than 143 different names:* PSSU, Hospital and Health Care Workers, Maine State Employees, Oregon Public Employees, Los Angeles County Employees Association, and the list of variations kept right on going. Every local union had the autonomy to use its own name, its own colors, and its own logo. It was no surprise that I was constantly barraged by our own leaders as to why SEIU's name recognition was so low compared to the steel-workers', autoworkers', or teachers' unions.

We knew it would be hard to ask 143 different organizations, each with its own history and pride, to voluntarily change their identities. We adopted a purple-and-gold logo designed by SEIU's Mackie Lopez and offered free stationery, T-shirts, and redesign services to any local unions that chose to convert to the new look. Over time, more locals adopted the SEIU purple brand and changed their stationery and colors, and, in 2004, the convention delegates constitutionally required that the SEIU name be included in the official names of all local unions. Now every local union was part of the "purple army." I have more purple shirts than I care to admit and wear one most days for brand loyalty, but this process helped infuse in our local unions and members pride and SEIU unity across the nation. Our catalog of purple products, which includes bowling balls, megaphones, and clothing, has produced sales of over $2 million in a single year. All across the country, a gathering of purple at rallies or political events is a good sign that SEIU is in the house.

SEIU's laser focus on organizing created a more powerful champion for the workers it represents. In 1996, SEIU had 1.1 million members and was the fourth-largest union in the AFL-CIO. In 2000, SEIU had gained 300,000 new members, for a total membership of 1.4 million.

When I informed our convention delegates in Pittsburgh in 2004 that the union that used to be known as SEIwho? was now the largest labor union in the AFL-CIO, the room exploded with shrieks of joy. Confetti canons were shot off, music was played, and people danced in the aisles for nearly ten minutes.

SEIU, a union founded by powerless, low-wage immigrant janitors was once virtually unknown in an era of the industrial union legends. Now the voice of low-wage service workers in America is growing stronger every day because of the changes we instituted. And our members' lives are better for it.

Over the next four years, SEIU gained another 300,000 members, for an overall total membership of 1.7 million, and our margin increased significantly over the second-largest union in the AFL-CIO. SEIU's best year yet was 2005, when we gained union representation for an additional 200,000 workers and are closing in on becoming 2 million members strong.

I speak from experience when I say that a revived labor movement is the key to protecting workers against the downward spiral and the social costs of globalization. And, as someone who has pushed change through, I know it is possible—in even the most unlikely institutions. America needs a modern, pro-growth, dynamic, progressive, problem-solving labor movement, but we have a long way to go.

CHAPTER FIVE

Taking It to the Next Level

I am often asked: Why did SEIU take the radical step of breaking away from the AFL-CIO? Didn't you weaken the labor movement rather than strengthen it? Doesn't SEIU's withdrawal reveal fissures rather than present a unified front? SEIU's decision to leave the AFL-CIO was analyzed and interpreted both within and outside the labor movement. SEIU's critics emerged from all quarters. I was taken to the woodshed for every excuse under the sun: for the very act of making the suggestions for change; for making them before the November elections; for being arrogant, undemocratic, and selfish; for publicly surfacing labor's problems; for being disloyal to John Sweeney.

The answer to those criticisms is that most union's and the AFL-CIO's refusal to embrace the kind of structural changes that we have implemented to such powerful effect at SEIU is weakening the labor movement. We at SEIU and the other unions who broke away from the AFL-CIO and founded the Change to Win Federation in September 2005 did so because the leadership of the AFL-CIO refused to recognize what needed to be done to gain new strength for workers in the twenty-first century. Most unions preferred to resist reform rather than accept the harder task of persuading their members to accept the changes that would make the labor movement the vigorous, compelling force it once was and could be again. The labor movement should play a catalytic role in pushing through the economic and political reforms that are needed to contend with the challenges of globalization, reforms that will benefit workers, business and entire communities.

The break was necessary because of three key failures on the part of the AFL-CIO to help American workers: one, to confront its own underlying structural impediments and those of its affiliates; two, to refocus on membership growth; and three, to modernize its strategic approaches to employers in order to take into account their competitive business needs. The story of the founding of the Change to Win Federation speaks volumes about why the labor union membership has been in such dramatic decline in recent decades and about why radical evolution is possible in the movement.

I made the commitment to either force change in the AFL-CIO or to opt to form a new federation with eight words in a speech I gave at the SEIU's quadrennial convention in San Francisco in June 2004: *either change the AFL-CIO—or build something stronger.*

At SEIU, we had learned that you can't always control the exact course of reform, but if you remain steadfast to your vision you will end up in a far better place than you started. In the eight years since our historic convention in 1996 in Chicago, we'd grown from 1.1 million members to 1.7 million members. While most Americans were losing or paying more for their health care, our janitors and home care and child care workers were gaining it. In markets like New Jersey, janitors saw hourly wage increases of four to five dollars in their first contract—a nearly 80 percent increase in three years. Nurses were winning quality care through safe staffing committees, and health care workers and security officers were gaining enhanced training and promotion funds.

The leadership of SEIU realized that the more the larger union population adopted the kinds of changes we had made, the more powerful the whole movement would become, thus reinvigorating the role of the labor movement in our economic and political systems. We spent two years reviewing the elements of SEIU's success and assessing whether or not our strategies could be adopted successfully by other unions, and we decided that not only could they, but that doing so was urgent.

Virtually every single day that I worked with the AFL-CIO, it represented a smaller and smaller portion of the workforce — the very source of its strength. It became increasingly irrelevant to its remaining members, and the signs became obvious that a shrinking movement had become less relevant to the economy and the changes confronting the workforce at the exact time when the disparity of wealth, the decline in health care coverage and retirement security, and stagnant wages demanded labor's relevance even more.

It did not take sophisticated research to realize that America's future would not rest on a mass-production, industrial base and that more and more employers were transforming themselves from national companies to international ones. Yet most unions refused to adapt, preferring to blame their diminishing strength on politicians, employers, trade agreements, and even other unions. To quote Bob Dylan: "He not busy being born is busy dying." Rebirth was not on the union agenda.

As SEIU's representative to the AFL-CIO Executive Council, its top decision-making body, I had attended its meetings for ten years and led several key committees. I was privy to the private discussions among the national leaders regarding the labor movement's decline. As the initial momentum begun by President Sweeney faltered at the AFL-CIO and our candidate lost the 2000 presidential election, that internal criticism increased. Along with others, I offered suggestions and made formal proposals, only to watch as nothing changed.

The AFL-CIO refused to acknowledge the movement's complicity in its failings: We were really *dis*organized labor. For example, the thirteen unions operating in the airline industry often would not coordinate with one another. Twelve different unions tried to organize hotel workers. No fewer than thirty separate unions attempted to organize health care workers. On construction sites, employers had to contend with fifteen building-trade unions divided into narrow, archaic craft jurisdictions that technology and other new work processes had rendered obsolete. This overlap created confusion, unnecessary competition, and conflicting approaches to the same employer.

The AFL-CIO was willing to identify these structural problems in the union movement, but the overriding obstacle was that the leadership was unwilling to address the problems. Several studies during Lane Kirkland's presidency of the AFL-CIO indicated the need for change, including the 1983 report "The Future of Work," which looked at employment patterns and the effects of emerging technology on work. This report led to a blueprint for increasing labor's influence, issued in 1985, titled "The Changing Situation of Workers and Their Unions," which called for structural changes and mergers.

A later study of trends in membership and changes in employment patterns instigated by John Sweeney analyzed the major sectors of the economy and projections of job growth. It again demonstrated that unionized sectors were losing jobs faster than average while nonunion sectors were gaining above average. The report identified the "lead" unions in each sector and implied strongly that those unions should be responsible for sectoral bargaining, growth plans, and employer relationships. The report also suggested that other unions should merge their members into a "lead" union or, at a minimum, halt further growth efforts in those areas. It was a road map for change that was completely ignored. Despite all evidence to the contrary, many union leaders preferred to contend that there was no crisis. And why not? Their members were not demanding fundamental change. These leaders earned good salaries, had secure pensions, and had expense accounts at their disposal. They were consulted and treated as power players by elected officials and the Democratic Party.

If the only consequences of our failure to respond to the tide of history were that union leaders lost their jobs and put their headquarters up for sale, that might be just fine, and the union movement might be justly remembered as an institution whose time had simply come and gone. But in what is becoming a winner-take-all economy, the declining strength of unions means that American workers pay an unacceptable price.

For a time after John Sweeney's election in 1995 as AFL-CIO president, it seemed that the AFL-CIO was heading in the right direction. The most significant step forward was a revitalized political program initiated by President Sweeney. Steve Rosenthal, then political director of the AFL-CIO, and Gerry McEntee, then chair of the Political Committee, successfully rebuilt labor's political prowess. They switched the focus of the political program from one of an open cash register for candidates to one that mobilized members to political action and raised the profile of issues important to members. In California, the labor movement beat back Proposition 226, which would have significantly reduced unions' ability to participate in the political process. We also helped elect a governor, Gray Davis, who was considered "road kill" by the pundits. In 1996, labor helped defeat nineteen of Newt Gingrich's protégés, contributing to Gingrich's unraveling. The AFL-CIO started the "2000 in 2000" program to elect union members to public office; its goal was exceeded and more than two thousand union members were elected to public office. Finally, also in 2000, the labor movement's early support of Vice President Gore in Iowa and New Hampshire helped secure him the nomination.

The AFL-CIO renewed its political clout, and politicians not only listened more carefully to what we said, they attentively watched what we did. In the 1992 U.S. presidential election, the turnout of union members was no higher than their proportion in the electorate. However, in 1996, the political program showed its force: While only 16 percent of eligible voters came from union households, of those who actually voted in the election, 23 percent were from union homes. In the 2000 presidential election, while union households represented only 15 percent of the electorate, they produced 26 percent of the voters. If only there had been more union members in Ohio and Florida, the last two presidential elections might have turned out differently.

However, if we simply continued to apply that newfound power, given labor's ever-shrinking membership base, our vaunted political program would yield increasingly diminishing returns. Additional changes were clearly required. Although acutely aware of the movement's decline, President Sweeney wanted to avoid contentious debates and suggested only superficial changes. In the final analysis, he placed a higher premium on unity than on change, which ironically forced the issue of SEIU's breakaway.

Up to this time, SEIU had worked only on its own major internal remodeling, and had only perfunctorily attempted to promote change within the AFL-CIO. When it became clear that reform within the AFL-CIO was stalled, SEIU's leaders realized that it was irresponsible to just stand by and watch the living standards of American workers decline. It was time to walk down a different road.

I did not make the decision to force the issue of reform lightly. I had enormous respect for John Sweeney, his union career, and his many accomplishments. The decision was excruciating.

I've learned that sometimes in life, we have to experience a life-shattering event to empower us to reevaluate our priorities. At least that's the way it was with me. I went through just that kind of experience the year leading up to my speech at the SEIU Convention when I challenged the AFL-CIO. I honestly don't know if I would have had the determination or conviction to confront the AFL-CIO if I hadn't been through the pain of the most devastating loss in my life.

We all know that the best moments in life are the ones spent with family, friends, spouses, and partners, reading the paper together on a Sunday morning, bike riding, taking vacations, eating a quiet meal, or just hanging out. The times when your baby crawls onto your lap to cuddle or you roughhouse with your kids on the living room floor. Those are moments you want to savor because life can deal you instant and irrevocable blows.

I know. Four years ago, at age thirteen, my daughter, Cassie, died in my arms and shattered my world.

I love being a father. My devotion to my work could never compete with my love of being the dad to my two adopted children, Cassie and Matt. They have been the center of my life.

Despite superb medical care from birth, Cassie confronted health issues we never completely understood. She had very weak muscle tone, developed slowly, and could not gain weight; she also developed scoliosis, an abnormal curvature of the spine. Ensure, vitamins, high-calorie diets, and other "cures" were a regular part of our life, but at thirteen she was only four feet eight inches tall and struggled to crack the sixty-pound mark. She compensated for her small size by being the most determined person I have ever met. She would ask anything, argue about everything, and she never gave ground.

For several years after she developed scoliosis she wore a back brace in an attempt to retard the curvature of the spine. She couldn't participate in sports or most of the activities in gym class, but she always suited up. Too many times, she got stuck in the ladies' room because the doors took more force to open than she could muster.

At the New Jersey shore, where we often went for vacations, Cassie couldn't handle the power of the ocean's waves: She would run toward the water, but as soon as the waves ran over her feet, she would race back to dry shore. Even at the age of thirteen, she would let me stand behind her, holding her hands in the air so I could lift her, screaming with joy, over the waves as they crashed onto the shore.

I often took Matt and Cassie on adventures, sometimes together, often separately, so we could spend rare time alone. In Rome, on Easter Sunday of the millennium, Cassie and I celebrated Papal Mass and then traveled on to Venice for an evening ride in a gondola. One year, Matt and I went scuba diving in Australia, explored New Zealand's rain forests, and survived a hair-raising ride to Cairns on the "wrong" side of the road. We took countless trips, touring America from coast to coast and border to border, including special adventures in a Winnebago, which Matt always called his "camper truck." I was the recipient of family abuse for years for miscalculating the width of the Winnebago and ripping the bumper off at the first refueling.

When Cassie was twelve, she was invited by her best friend, Moneyi, to visit her grandparents in Botswana. It may have been divine intervention that I was scheduled to visit South Africa at the same time. I met Cassie, Moneyi, and Moneyi's mom, Joyce, at the Johannesburg airport and drove with them to their family home in Botswana, where we were greeted by goats grazing in the front yard. We found accommodations that were spartan by American standards—a wood stove, three guests to one mattress—but a home filled with comfort, love, and grace. Cassie either ignored or was unfazed by the fact that she was the only white child for miles.

After staying overnight, Cassie, Moneyi, and I drove north to a game preserve before a breathtaking visit to Victoria Falls. Delayed by a magnificent crossing of a herd of elephants, we arrived in time for a dinner that included antelope, fried caterpillars, and unidentified tubers. Cassie tasted everything.

We awoke early the next morning and set off on safari in our open-top jeep; we passed lions eating antelope and giraffes feeding on treetops. At the end of the day, we took a boat ride on a lake. As Cassie leaned into my arms, elephants burst out of the jungle and splashed in the water, hippos lolled on the bank, and an outsized, fulvous red sun set over the horizon. It was blissful, and I whispered to Cassie, "Sweetheart, it doesn't get much better than this!" I had no idea that that trip would be our last.

The brace was not successful in halting Cassie's scoliosis and she was forced to undergo two surgeries. After ten days of recovery from her second surgery, at NYU Medical Center,

Cassie's doctor pronounced her well enough to travel to our annual Memorial Day weekend at the beach.

I had taken to staying by Cassie's side as she slept, and, in the middle of the night shortly after her release from the hospital, I woke up. With a parent's sixth sense, I felt that something was wrong. As I listened in the darkness, I realized with horror that she had stopped breathing. In seconds, my life had become a living nightmare.

Frantically, I called for help, and tried to keep her alive until the ambulance arrived by administering mouth-to-mouth resuscitation. She was rushed by the EMTs to Somers Memorial Hospital in Somers Point, while I drove like a madman yards behind the ambulance. In the emergency room, I waited and waited and waited until finally the nurse came out and informed me that Cassie was dead.

As I called my wife—to deliver the worst news a parent can—the nurse suddenly returned to report what seemed like miracle. A faint heartbeat had been detected: Cassie was still fighting.

Cassie was in a coma, and the doctors decided that she should be helicoptered to Children's Hospital in Philadelphia, where she was rushed to a special unit where they packed her body in ice to try to arrest brain damage. When they unchilled her body a day later, however, there was no brain activity.

Within hours, my family mobilized and poured into Philadelphia. Cassie's world-class surgeon and her pediatrician rushed to join us, incredulous because this was not supposed to have happened. Cassie's friends and their families joined the vigil.

During those days, we existed in a surreal bubble that consisted of the hospital waiting room, one lone hallway, and Cassie's room. As time passed with no improvement, the searing reality became clear—my wife Jane, Matt, and I had to figure out how to say goodbye.

The doctors talked us through the medical protocols involved in separating Cassie from life support and, with only the doctor in the room to free Cassie from the machines that kept her alive, Jane and I wrapped our arms around her and within minutes she died in our embrace.

There is no way to prepare yourself for your child's death. Human brains are simply not wired to deal with the loss. It is inconceivable, a pain that cannot be imagined. One moment you think you have so much and then it's gone—forever. After Cassie died, I saved the hair bands that her friends had braided into her hair, which she wore on her last day, and I have worn one on my little finger ever since. I kiss them often—when a memory or another child reminds me of her—and I know that someday I will feel her love more than the loss.

Thank God for Matt. He is what I live for; he is proof of the future. His "What's up, Pops?" greeting never fails to bring a smile to my face, and the hugs I get from him every day I am with him are fuel for my heart.

With time, my loss of Cassie began to transform the way I approached life. Her death challenged me to look deeply inside myself and ask hard questions about my beliefs and my fears. That questioning made me more determined to confront challenges head-on, and to make the most of the gift of living and to fight with that much more determination for the things that really matter in life. Cassie's death became the fountain of courage in my life.

Her courage was with me when I stepped up to the podium at the SEIU Convention that June 2004. I was prepared to make one of the most difficult decisions I've made in my work life, but one that I had considered with the thoroughness it deserved. I was simply too aware of how pressing the challenges that confronted the labor movement were to fail to take that decisive step.

I issued a public challenge that day, a clear ultimatum to the leaders of the AFL-CIO—change, or SEIU would leave to build a new and stronger labor organization. I proposed the following. Change from a loose trade association of sixty-five separate and autonomous unions into a strong, united organization;

reorganize its structure by restricting each union to organize only within its own industry; merge unions where industry overlap occurred; create enforceable standards to stop unions from conspiring with employers against other unions; build stronger global alliances.

SEIU's delegates supported the call for change, responding enthusiastically with a standing ovation and thundering applause. However, once the challenge was reported in the press, alarm bells rang throughout the labor movement and Democratic Washington.

With the 2004 U.S. presidential election as our backdrop, John Sweeney and I met in September to discuss SEIU's ideas for reforming the AFL-CIO. At our initial meeting, I outlined my broad concerns and described SEIU's solutions. John was no stranger to our proposals, since most mirrored the changes and resultant successes within SEIU that he had instigated and watched blossom over the last ten years.

I had approached John out of both personal respect and an understanding that if the change process was led by the president of the organization, its odds of success would be exponentially increased. I also knew that after nine years as president of the AFL-CIO, John would have his own insights, thoughts, and specific ideas regarding a framework for change. I was prepared to be flexible in modifying SEIU's plans if he would accept the leadership. John listened patiently, and while he offered no specific reforms, he suggested forming a small working group to find common ground.

The first discussion of that group exposed no real differences in everyone's views regarding the problems facing the labor movement. John's representatives agreed with the sensibility of our suggestions, but they argued repeatedly about each one's practicality, countering that many unions within the AFL-CIO would oppose the direction of SEIU's changes.

Ultimately, the AFL-CIO leadership produced no proposal for change, and SEIU prepared to release our own plan. We waited to do so until after the November elections; SEIU had worked hard to contribute to the labor movement's efforts to support a Democratic Party victory and we didn't want to undermine those efforts.

SEIU's comprehensive proposals called for the following:

- Structural alterations to the labor movement to promote industry concentration by reducing the number of AFL-CIO affiliates from sixty-five to approximately twenty, focusing each union on a major sector of the economy.
- Coordinated approaches and bargaining among employees working for the same employer or in the same industry.
- The return of 50 percent of their AFL-CIO dues to industry-focused unions that had an approved strategic growth plan. This is what came to be known as the "50 percent rebate."
- Discussions with unions overseas about global union alliances.
- Campaigns to stop the Wal-Marting—low pay and few benefits—of American jobs and to promote affordable health care and the free choice of workers to join unions.
- The establishment of unions in the new knowledge and technology sectors where none were active; shifting resources to the country's areas of growth, the South and the Southwest.
- A new focus on grassroots activity of AFL-CIO state and local labor federations and member involvement in electoral political activity.
- Greater diversity and accountability in leadership.

The proposal to restructure and reduce the number of unions by industry was considered a frontal assault on the unions' independence and drew the fiercest reactions. The suggestion was decimated without debate. Behind each possible merged union was a leader with a good job and an impressive title— neither of which would be relinquished peacefully.

The struggle was reminiscent of a longtime debate that

stretched across the history of the AFL-CIO. The AFL was created in 1886 by skilled workers—carpenters, shoemakers, printers, machinists, locomotive engineers, and others—who wanted to be organized by their crafts. As the industrial economy grew in new mass-production industries, such as automobile and steel manufacturing, the AFL continued the same strategy of allowing each craft union to organize just the particular piece of the employer most closely aligned to their craft's skills.

The CIO was formed first as the Committee of Industrial Organizations within the AFL in 1935, and in 1938 the CIO left the AFL (and became the Congress of Industrial Organizations). The raging debate that resulted in the CIO's departure was about how best to strategically respond to the budding mass-production industrial economy—a striking parallel to the discussion that we were having almost seventy years later. The CIO strategy posited that for each employer and each industry there should be only one union. They believed that dividing the strength of workers into multiple crafts was an inherently weak strategy, which would require unnecessary and time-consuming union coordination or, more destructive, conflicting strategies in the same industry.

John L. Lewis, president of the newly formed CIO, created a series of industrial organizing committees and launched campaigns to unionize GM, U.S. Steel, Ford, Chrysler, and textile employers. The competition between the AFL and the CIO began, and it served American workers well because both federations spent large sums of money on organizing new members. It was in this period that union membership reached its historic peak.

By the 1940s, both the AFL and CIO had become important pillars in America, its leaders consulted by presidents on national issues. Yet, in the more stable, post-WWII environment, the affiliates' leaders lost their passion for growth and the desire for ongoing labor competition. Eager to enjoy their newfound success, and suffering from selective amnesia about the differences that had led to their separation, the AFL and CIO merged in 1955—*without reconciling the underlying structural dilemma of craft versus industry unionism.*

To protect the autonomy of each affiliate and to ensure that the new federation would have no constitutional authority over any affiliate, the AFL-CIO's first constitution enshrined this fateful language: "The Federation shall be composed of: (1) national and international unions that are affiliated with, but *are not subordinate to* [emphasis added], or subject to the general direction and control of, the Federation." And to protect each union's existing membership, raiding another union's existing members was outlawed.

The next three decades of the union movement was dominated by formal labor-management dispute-resolution mechanisms with an emphasis on representing workers who were already in unions and voted in union elections. The time was also hallmarked by a more professional administration and a less confrontational style in employer relations, which some described as "business unionism."

With no requirements limiting unions to organize only within their existing industry jurisdiction, and new protections against union raiding, unions expanded into new areas where organizing was easier, such as the public sector and the hotel industry. In addition, employers would intentionally invite unions to organize their workers with the hope that the new union would undermine an existing, stronger union. Or a union might simply respond to a random phone call from a worker in a different industry rather than refer the call to the appropriate union in that sector.

Lines blurred, new unions entered old industries, and strategic coordination became nearly impossible as each union pursued its plans alone and unencumbered by structural guidelines. The de-emphasis on gaining new members led to a sustained loss of union density, but still no union leader wanted to change the status quo.

✳   ✳   ✳

SEIU mailed our reform proposal to the national unions and to the state and local AFL-CIO affiliate unions. We created a Web site and I began to blog. People responded and the public debate began in earnest.

It was not a happy time in certain segments of the Washington labor community. I was bludgeoned by colleagues who would have preferred I disappeared or, at the very least, confined my remarks to the closed sanctuary of the AFL-CIO Executive Council. As is often the case, the media prefer stories that center on conflict and framed this story accordingly. The appeal of a union "split," or the psychodramatic, Oedipal story of Andy Stern betraying his mentor John Sweeney, or other leaders extolling their impression of my numerous personality flaws was too hard for reporters to resist. But the winds of change started to blow.

In December, we got a jolt of momentum when the Teamsters, not a historic ally of SEIU, sent shock waves throughout the union movement by releasing a proposal that had been endorsed by President Hoffa and the entire Teamsters Executive Board. The 1.4 million Teamsters added new dimensions to the debate and reinforced many of the key SEIU proposals—specifically the 50 percent rebate plan. At a time when garnering membership was the missing initiative in most unions, SEIU and the Teamsters agreed that money being sent to the AFL-CIO could more effectively be used by individual unions to grow—*but only if their growth efforts were applied to assigned industries and industry sectors.* In order for unions to get the rebate, the Teamsters' proposal required unions to develop a plan outlining their strategy, which would include an annual investment of either 10 percent of their own budgets or at least $2 million. When the union's plan was approved by the AFL-CIO, it would return to the union half of its payments to the federation. It was a thoughtful and progressive proposal and one that made the AFL-CIO's strategy to isolate SEIU impossible.

Rather than respond to the specifics of the plan, many

national leaders cynically called the rebate proposal a Trojan horse designed to dismantle the five-hundred-plus AFL-CIO bureaucracy and reduce services to smaller national unions. With the major unions advocating change, the floodgates opened and more reform proposals followed: from the United Food and Commercial Workers (UFCW), the Firefighters, the Laborers, and the AFL-CIO Building Trades Department. When the dust settled there were over twenty-eight proposals submitted.

The discussion that ensued was healthy, pitting those who felt a compelling need to confront the evolving economic world openly against the immovable institutional force of the national labor movement—a battle that was necessary and long overdue. But President Sweeney continued his pattern of leading from the center, trying to close debate and build a consensus by appealing for unity.

At the March 2005 meeting of the AFL-CIO Executive Council, however, the Sweeney forces switched strategies and executed a time-honored power play. Prior to the full fifty-four-member Executive Council Meeting, the smaller Executive Committee of twenty-five met. Throwing consensus to the wind, the AFL-CIO leadership orchestrated a surprise vote on the Teamsters' 50 percent rebate proposal. This was politics at its most savvy: If you know you've got the votes, roll your opposition; put a motion on the floor, call for the end of debate, and take the vote to show who is in control. The 50 percent rebate lost, fifteen to seven, but the AFL-CIO's move marked a turning point for a number of union leaders, including Joe Hansen of the United Food and Commercial Workers (UFCW), Jim Hoffa of the Teamsters, Terry O'Sullivan of the Laborer's President, and Bruce Raynor and John Wilhelm of UNITE HERE. These five union leaders, joined by Anna Burger, secretary-treasurer of SEIU, and myself, held a joint press conference where we publicly expressed our disappointment with our colleagues' show of force. But, more important, for the first time, we offered a joint vision for a new labor federation. We pledged to form an alliance and merge our multiple proposals into one set of recommendations.

As the AFL-CIO meetings progressed over the course of the weekend, other union leaders explained their opposition to a growth agenda. Leo Gerard, president of the Steelworkers, for example, shared the story of his union's failed investment in organizing—of all sectors to highlight—health care. *Steelworkers failing to organize health care workers.* Gerard unexpectedly and ironically reinforced SEIU's concern over the labor movement's disarray.

However, the lesson Gerard took from his inability to organize health care workers was that the labor movement's greatest success resided in electing friendly politicians who would in turn improve labor laws to make them more supportive of America's workers. Gerard had concluded that investing in growth had no payoff. It was the old chicken-and-egg question: change the political process before you could grow stronger or grow stronger to change the political process. Unions had been waiting for a long time for Democrats to rescue us. Despite four Democratic presidents since the AFL-CIO's inception, and decades of a Democratic-controlled Congress, the union movement had steadily lost members. Hitching our fate to politics and Democratic politicians had proved to be a losing strategy for American workers.

In a public relations campaign, the AFL-CIO purposefully misrepresented our new alliance's position as abandoning politics to focus solely on organizing. Sweeney and his partisans were acutely aware that SEIU, in addition to lobbying for changes in labor laws, had been asking elected officials for years to personally support our organizing campaigns, to impressive effect. Governor Blagojevich (Illinois), Governor Gregoire (Washington), Governor Kulongoski (Oregon), Governor Pataki (New York), Mayor Hahn (Los Angeles), Mayor Bloomberg (New York City), and former Governor Davis (California) had helped our mostly low-wage workers have a choice regarding union representation.

In New Haven, Connecticut, U.S. Representative Rosa

DeLauro and Mayor John DeStefano helped SEIU resolve a dispute at Yale-New Haven Hospital. New York State's Governor George Pataki signed a bill that allowed public workers to have a union without having to endure traditional work-site wars. School boards in Texas, city councils in Arizona, and Mayor Bill White in Houston had all chosen to give workers the opportunity to vote freely on union representation, and electoral politics had become a key component in our growth strategies. Organizing and politics, we extolled, were two sides of the same coin. Increased membership permitted us to gain strength in the short run to change public policy in the long run. But the AFL-CIO leadership chose to disregard our arguments and ignore two of the most basic tenets of the federation's mission—to keep unions from interfering with other unions' organizing and to promote membership growth.

For ten years, SEIU had been organizing forty-nine thousand Illinois private-sector family child care providers, mostly women and people of color, who provide day care in their homes, allowing other low-wage parents to work. Women like Angenita Tanner, from Chicago, lovingly cared for the children in her care. Her all too typical net pay of six to seven dollars per hour with no benefits inspired lawmakers to take action. SEIU's Illinois union had built a powerful base of support among the workers, but it took a progressive new governor to issue an executive order to allow the workers to lawfully create a union that could bargain with the Illinois State government over child care reimbursement rates.

Ten years of intensive work had put us on the verge of a historic breakthrough when an AFL-CIO affiliate union, AFSCME, unexpectedly filed a lawsuit that, had it been successful, would have invalidated that executive order, derailing SEIU's efforts. After twenty years of inaction, AFSCME was trying to take advantage of our hard work to gain new members for its own union, actions that could result in the workers ending up with no union whatsoever.

I was livid, and at that March meeting of the AFL-CIO

Executive Committee I called on President Sweeney to demand that AFSCME withdraw their lawsuit. In a too typical example of labor's inability to honorably address its flaws, President Sweeney said only that he would look into it. It was unfathomable to me that the AFL-CIO, safely ensconced in a fancy hotel in Las Vegas, would ask for time to investigate while Illinois workers, who were only trying to ensure that their work was rewarded with fair pay, were being pulled in different directions by two competing unions.

AFSCME's campaign with the child care providers never got off the ground. They lost their lawsuit and withdrew days before an overwhelming yes vote for SEIU. The Illinois experience further solidified our desire to leave an institution where members' interests took a backseat to union politics.

The fissures that appeared in March began to clarify for all five unions that eventually joined SEIU, the consequences for each union of our collective failure to change the AFL-CIO. SEIU would withdraw from the federation and then each union would be similarly confronted with the decision to remain affiliated or leave.

Private deals were offered by the AFL-CIO leadership to entice the union presidents to break from our fledgling coalition. Threats were also made: As part of an effort to force our unions to stay in the AFL-CIO, some union presidents threatened to withdraw their money from the only union bank in America owned by UNITE HERE.

Yet the five unions had been holding fruitful discussions steadily since March, and we were homing in on the strategic questions we needed to answer. Even if we were able to gain the votes to reform the AFL-CIO, why would we reelect John Sweeney as president to implement a program we knew he opposed? And if not Sweeney, who would be our candidate? SEIU had already concluded that reforming the AFL-CIO required both the right program and the right leader. Other unions wondered if there was middle ground.

Another question was equally complicated: Should we attend the AFL-CIO Convention when the standing rules of procedure for the convention made a fair debate and decision-making process unattainable? Our unions had fully 40 percent of the AFL-CIO's membership, but because of the rules of the convention we had only 9 percent of the voting delegates.

To date, our five unions had operated in an ad hoc alliance, but it had become clear that it was important to formalize our coalition to cement and maintain our new alliance regardless of the AFL-CIO reform results. On June 15, 2005, at the Laborers International Union Headquarters, across the street from the AFL-CIO headquarters, I stood with the presidents of the Teamsters, Laborers, UFCW, and UNITE HERE to announce the formation of the Change to Win Coalition, creating a permanent organization, one important step shy of a formal break, thus from the AFL-CIO. Nonetheless, we hoped that these concrete proposals would make a difference in the thinking of the AFL-CIO leadership.

We proposed mandatory rules to prohibit one union from undermining another in contract standards, and to enforce coordinated bargaining, whereas the AFL-CIO had proposed only voluntary ones.

Our proposal called for incentives for unions to merge; the AFL-CIO plan didn't address the issue of mergers.

Our proposal called for national standards of accountability for all affiliates who had an AFL-CIO charter; theirs continued to grant autonomy to each AFL-CIO union, which would result in the AFL-CIO continuing its lowest-common-denominator approach.

Where our proposal used the word *must*, theirs used the word *may*. Where we said *mandatory*, they said *voluntary*. That was the crux of the difference.

As we arrived in Chicago for the AFL-CIO's fiftieth-anniversary convention on July 25, 2005, we were informed privately that John Sweeney had offered to resign if that would keep the five unions within the AFL-CIO. It was a noble gesture, but his resignation would not have solved the underlying problems.

The 1995 election of President Sweeney had proved that a leadership transition without accompanying restructuring would not turn the AFL-CIO around. And certainly for the Change to Win unions, remaining in the AFL-CIO with no structural change and an unknown replacement for president was not an option.

Over the course of three decades in the labor movement I had watched its overall steady decline while looking for signs of movement-wide rejuvenation. During my days I fulfilled my leadership role of trying to help the lives of American workers. But at night I wondered if I had the courage to take the actions to halt the decline of the labor movement I loved.

As I stood at the podium that July day in Chicago to give my speech announcing that SEIU would not attend the AFL-CIO convention, I thought back to the moment in San Francisco one year earlier, when I had stood alone on the SEIU Convention stage, nervous before finding my voice, to call for change. One year later, I was standing with five other unions, collectively representing nearly 6 million workers, with hope that we could forge a new path for American workers. Big changes begin with small steps.

The next morning, Teamster president Jimmy Hoffa and I delivered letters to John Sweeney and held a joint press conference announcing our decision to leave the AFL-CIO. In my letter, I wrote that if there comes a point when we can't reach agreement on very basic principles, we should respectfully accept our differences, and chart our own separate futures. It was a bittersweet moment, but after eighty-four years of SEIU's membership in the AFL-CIO, ten years of discussion, and eight months of concerted but failed efforts to make change—it was time.

The unions of the Change to Win Coalition, now joined by Doug McCarron and the Carpenters Union that had left the AFL-CIO years earlier, and Arturo Rodriquez of the Farmworkers Union, agreed to create the first new labor federation in America in fifty years.

The leaders of the new Change to Win Federation approved the establishment of a new Strategic Organizing Center, led by SEIU's Tom Woodruff and funded by 75 percent of Change to Win's income from dues, to centralize the functions and resources that would be needed to execute new and larger growth campaigns.

We agreed to develop procedures that directed each union's organizing efforts on their key industries and not each other's.

Change to Win's founding convention in September in St. Louis was historic and spiritually refreshing as members approved a constitution and elected SEIU's Secretary-Treasurer Anna Burger as Chair, the first woman ever to lead an American labor federation.

Six months later, Change to Win was cooking. We held the largest organizing conference in modern labor history, where two thousand organizers and researchers met to share strategies and develop campaigns. We launched our first nationwide effort to spotlight the low wages and hard work of hotel workers, where the pay rates have no relationship to room rates, only to unionization rates. Under our new mantra, "Make Work Pay," we promised to be the voice for the millions of hardworking service workers in the industries our unions represented.

In the aftermath of SEIU's departure from the AFL-CIO, I often was congratulated for SEIU's role in the change process. While I felt as though we were establishing a new force for American workers, I always countered the congratulations with the truth: Leaving the AFL-CIO was not an accomplishment, only an opportunity. What is SEIU doing with that opportunity? Are we making our radical move worthwhile? Yes. SEIU is experimenting with bold new approaches that—if successful—will serve as the foundation for more effective twenty-first-century unions. Read on.

CHAPTER SIX

The Strength of One

If anyone had suggested to me a year ago that there was anything in the world on which Newt Gingrich and I would agree, I would have been offended at the very idea. When Gingrich was elected Speaker of the House of Representatives, I considered him the devil incarnate. And for good reason. He led a Congress that tried to dismantle every right and protection that unions had helped put in place for over fifty years—including the Davis-Bacon Act and the Service Contract Act. He attempted to pass two bills specifically targeted at weakening the labor movement, the Team Act and Paycheck Protection, both of which were vehemently opposed by labor. At the 2000 SEIU Convention, I fired up the crowd at his expense, remarking on his departure from Congress: "The flames burned Newt Gingrich and his Contract with America so bad that he left on the midnight train to Georgia." But almost a decade later, after an hour with Gingrich I was more than pleasantly surprised by his thoughtfulness and candor.

I first met Gingrich in Chicago at a Republican Main Street Partnership meeting, where Anna Burger, as chair of the Change to Win Federation, was scheduled to speak along with the former Speaker. We had coffee together before their presentations. Anna and I were surprised by Gingrich's smart and contemplative demeanor. As only a history scholar can, Gingrich talked in broad historical terms of the change-making process, the challenges facing our country, and America's need to confront its future.

Gingrich had been following the changes in the labor movement and saw the formation of the Change to Win Federation as part of the natural evolution of the industrial economy to one based on knowledge and service workers. He believes it is important that the labor movement and America help the bottom third of our society achieve middle-class incomes and lifestyles. In order to do so, he argued, labor would have to continually rethink its role in the changing economy — specifically, how it could deliver increased productivity and better services to its members and employers.

Gingrich's thinking reinforced much of my own. My efforts to make change within SEIU helped me to understand the necessity of continually reevaluating the union's role in its members' lives and its place with employers in our industries and within the overall economy, particularly as industries evolve. One evolving industry is real estate. Real estate ownership has evolved from individual wealthy owners to Real Estate Investment Trusts (REITs), companies that operate many types of income-producing real estate, such as hospitals, condominiums, shopping centers, and nursing home properties, whose shares often are traded on the stock exchange. As a consequence, our union's relationship with the "employer" must evolve accordingly.

Newt Gingrich talked about the process of institutional change and he launched into his lecturer's mode. He pulled out a set of diagrams he called *Designing Transformational Change* that communicate twelve steps to promote organizational transformation. He traced for us the steps in an organizational change process. His working proposition is that change is a learned and practiced behavior that requires planning, strategy, and leadership. The titles of some of the diagrams convey the flavor of his language: *Assert Truth; All Politics Is Personal; Focus on Offense Not Defense.*

Gingrich cited his respect for the United States Army as an institution that consciously and continuously conforms itself to changing times. The army's management accepts change as a fact of life and has worked for decades to reshape itself to meet changing security needs. It actually integrates change into its planning process.

Some wonder whether the army is to blame for the quagmire Iraq has become. Time has revealed that our political leaders rushed to war in Iraq without a plan and enough troops to secure peace—over the objections of many in the military, as some former generals have revealed. If the Iraq fiasco was the outcome of ineffective planning, then my guess is that the army will evaluate their planning process and make any necessary changes.

In the foreword to a new edition of Alvin and Heidi Toffler's 1995 book *Creating a New Civilization: The Politics of the Third Wave*, Gingrich wrote, "The new Army doctrine led to a more flexible, fast-paced, decentralized, information-rich system which assessed the battlefield, focused resources and utilized well-trained but very decentralized leadership to overwhelm an industrial-era opponent."

Unlike unions and political parties, Gingrich said that the army rigorously studies, evaluates, and makes regular adjustments to its long-term plans, and holds endless simulations to enhance its ability to respond to any contingency. That's why people talk of substituting the army for FEMA in responding to natural disasters. According to Gingrich, the question we should ask is not why the army has become effective, but why hasn't FEMA?

After our first conversation, Gingrich's parting gift was his diagrams with his handwritten comments. He followed up with a personally annotated version of Tofflers' *Creating a New Civilization*. I am fixated on its opening lines as a depiction of our world's current paradigm:

A new civilization is emerging in our lives, and blind men everywhere are trying to suppress it. This new civilization brings with it new family styles, changed ways of working, loving, and living, a new economy, new political conflicts, and beyond all this an altered consciousness as well.

Humanity faces a quantum leap forward. It faces the deepest social upheaval and creative restructuring of all time. Without clearly recognizing it, we are engaged in building a remarkable new civilization from the ground up.

Anyone who might long wistfully for a return to the New Deal policies of 1935 should consider that America today is as far from the time of FDR as the New Deal was from Abe Lincoln and the Civil War. America is at a profound crossroads. Our nation and its citizens have to make difficult economic choices with serious long-term consequences. These decisions matter.

We can ignore change. We can be the "blind men" trying to suppress it. We can fight it, and no doubt, sooner or later, get run over by it.

Or, we can embrace change and help shape it.

GROWING INDIVIDUAL CHOICE
AND PERSONAL CONTROL

A trend that Gingrich and sophisticated marketers believe is crucial to the future are the technological advances that have created a massive increase in individual choice and a desire for greater personal control over decision making. On the Internet, we can shop, date, play games such as fantasy football and poker, and talk through e-mail, IMs, and blogs. The Internet—Google, eBay—has changed our lives, and Americans like the changes. JupiterResearch forecasts that online retail spending, $95 billion in 2006, will increase to $144 billion in 2010. In 2005, an estimated $60 billion was gambled in online poker worldwide. In one year, from 2004 to 2005, there was an increase of 29 percent in the amount of money spent online in personal ads and dating, from $272.1 million to $351.9 million. Life meets us at our fingertips.

Americans' attitudes about the level of individual control they have over their lives extend beyond the technological. Young adults expect choices to be customized to their desires. They demand constant access to whatever they want, whenever they want it. They insist on being treated as individuals and, in return, they take responsibility for their choices. Travel plans can be made without human intervention. Clothes can be bought without entering a store. MySpace and LiveJournal—sites where millions of young people post personal information online to find romance and to communicate with friends—are replacing diaries, dances, and blind dates. Job-hunting services, college applications, and homework can be accessed when you wake up first thing in the morning and into the wee hours of the night.

Individuals have a broader array of individually tailored choices that are often more vibrant and personal and not limited by geography. TiVo offers personalized television viewing, and that, combined with cable's one-hundred-plus television channels, has put an end to the dominance of CBS, ABC, and NBC. The American Medical Association is challenged by smaller specialty and subspecialty professional groups. MoveOn.org's virtual organization challenges traditional political-ward bosses and party fund-raisers. Craigslist.org, a free service of job postings, cripples newspapers' classified ads, depriving the established print organizations of a major source of revenue. Expedia.com replaces travel agents.

A world of endless options and enhanced individual control stresses institutions accustomed to providing group rather than individual services to its constituents. The pressure is nondiscriminatory, affecting political parties, unions, automakers, churches, medical and bar associations, traditional nonprofits and advocacy groups, and synagogues.

Those institutions that have adapted are thriving in this new environment. The megachurch phenomenon is a living representation of an institution that has adapted to today's expectations for individuality and personal attention. Megachurches, defined as churches with over two thousand congregants, are the fastest-growing large institutions in America. In 1960, there were only sixteen churches with weekly attendance over two thousand; today, the number tops twelve hundred and it is still growing.

The megachurches have enormous influence, reaching well beyond their congregations. In 2005, *The New York Times* had on its best-seller list four books written by megachurch pastors. In fact, one of these books is the best-selling nonfiction hardcover book in U.S. history.

My recent visit to the Radiant Church in Surprise, Arizona, a megachurch with fifteen thousand members, began with coffee and doughnuts at outdoor tables. Pastor Rick presided over a fun and upbeat service; he told jokes and self-deprecating stories while the audience followed along, literally, with pencil in hand, filling in the blanks of the pastor's lesson on their own copies of that day's sermon. I visited four different children's services with live performances by young, hip pastors. The rooms bulged with excited kids fully entertained but learning at the same time. The experience included many of the accoutrements of a live rock-band concert, such as theatrically produced productions shown on big screens.

Some megachurches seem more like miniature department stores, selling food, clothes, and books, drawing up to thirty thousand congregants to a worship. But underneath the glitzy surface is a caring community. Many megachurches offer small affinity groups for cancer survivors, children with learning issues, divorcees, and singles. They arrange Bible studies and field trips. Churches adopt communities both in the United States and abroad to which they minister and provide services and resources. As union halls were once a center of work life, these churches have become a center not only of spiritual life but of family and community life as well.

Just like other mass organizations, unions need to recognize that they are not immune to forces of change. They too must adapt or they will become irrelevant or extinct. Their relationship with their members must evolve into one that is more personalized, individualized, and accessible. Future-oriented, problem-solving, member-connected unions in the twenty-first century will be better equipped to face the challenges of today's economy.

EFFECTIVE TWENTY-FIRST-CENTURY UNIONS

SEIU's last ten years of experimentation with value-added employer relationships has evolved into a set of principles for successful workers' organizations and a more responsible competitiveness for employers.

- Employees and employers need organizations that solve problems, not create them. In a fast-paced, competitive world, unions need to facilitate competition by leveling the playing field for all employers, not by simply raising the costs of doing business for unionized ones alone. Unions must be experts in providing benefits and training, facilitating job mobility, and assisting employers in overcoming unnecessary legislative and political obstacles to their success.
- Both employers and employees must begin with the presumption that all parties want a mutually beneficial relationship based on teamwork. Both parties should lead with the power of persuasion. Recently, we have begun to ask our employers to serve as our "reference" to other employers with whom we seek to partner; our current employers can vouch for our good-faith efforts to improve training or solve problems that are important for business success. We are appearing at trade association meetings and public forums to engage in direct exchanges with business leaders on future opportunities.

- Improved quality, increased corporate revenue, and increased workers' skills and opportunities should all lead to more equitably distributed financial rewards.
- Unions must be responsive to market and competitive dynamics and the changing workplace. They should focus on entire industries and not individual work sites and employers.
- Work is not monolithic and unions cannot be "one size fits all" organizations. Individual workers need a more personal relationship with their union—"a union of one."
- To maximize success, employee organizations need to be aligned with employers' market and industry structures and flexible enough to respond to ever-changing employer dynamics, and competent enough to be good partners.
- Effective unions in an international economy must be global.
- Employees need to have a meaningful and independent voice in their workplaces on issues of quality, training, efficiency, and fairness.
- New organizations are needed to assist American workers in self-managing their work lives.

SEIU has been implementing a series of national initiatives to test whether these principles resonate with employers and workers. These initiatives will be evaluated to determine their viability for both workers and employers.

- One such effort is SEIU's Nurse Alliance "Value Care, Value Nurses" campaign, which was created to share among nurses information regarding working conditions at the bedside. In selected markets, nurses are forming citywide committees to discuss the quality of health care in their community and the obstacles to better patient care and nurse retention. They are also investigating ways in which they can approach all the employers in their market about how they can make high-quality, affordable health care available in their community.

The nurses intend to lobby on behalf of legislation that protects nurses who speak out on behalf of their patients, to support tax breaks for better mechanical devices to reduce back injuries, and to reduce involuntary overtime that leads to overtired staff and reduced quality of care.

- Nursing home owners and SEIU leaders are formulating a new national labor-management committee and new state-based relationships to promote quality and employer economic stability. In California, the industry and union worked with the legislature on a plan to enhance quality in nursing homes, stabilize the workforce, and provide more resources for direct patient care. The alliance secured a $660 million state legislative appropriation, which dramatically altered the fundamentals of the industry.

- SEIU is pursuing nationwide agreements with home care providers that include quality and training goals. For too long, home care, the preferred treatment for most seniors, has received inadequate government attention. In many cases, there is insufficient industry oversight, resulting in inadequate background checks, a lack of basic training, certification, and career development, and employers without the professional management experience to serve the growing senior population. We have begun to work with state and local governments and employers to shift resources from institutional care, like nursing homes, to less expensive home-based care.

- With security companies nationally, SEIU is experimenting with the market competitive practices we pioneered in our New Jersey Justice for Janitors campaign. We agree not to begin bargaining until a majority of the companies in the market recognize SEIU as the bargaining agent and are prepared to enter the discussion which provides for a marketwide rather than a single-employer solution. SEIU is also trying to add value to union security companies by working with mayors, police, and fire chiefs on integrated approaches between the building security and emergency responders to ensure that union security officers have the training, credentials, and knowledge to maximize safety in a post-9/11 world.

- SEIU forges new relationships with hospitals to mirror Kaiser and Catholic Healthcare West *before* any contentious organizing begins. In Allina Hospital in Minnesota, we mirrored other strategic hospital alliances and now hope to work with hospitals in a similar fashion in Massachusetts, Florida, and Maryland. We work out a set of protocols to assume there is a fast and fair way for workers to organize and avoid the contentious campaigns of the past.

These are all new tracks for our union to walk down, and we will see what the light is at the end of the tunnel: either new employer-employee relationships or the oncoming headlights of employers who see an opportunity to run workers over.

A New Old Role for Unions—Outsourcers

It took an invitation from the Human Resource Outsourcing Association to address their conference titled "Is Outsourcing the New Union Movement?" for me to realize the good sense of revitalizing an old union role.

Unions as outsourcers is not a novel concept. The fifteen building-trades unions have, in essence, been outsourcers for a long time; the process just hasn't been described that way. Employers turn to these unions to hire, train, and dispatch skilled craftspersons from their union halls to their job sites. Employers outsource benefits administration to the union—a defined per-hour contribution for health care and pension benefits—while workers are employed on their construction projects. When each job is completed, employers "return" the employees to the union hall until their next project, when the cycle begins again. This system provides benefits to both employers and employees: Employers gain flexibility and workers gain continuity in the management of their benefits.

So why can't all unions be "outsourcers" in this way, for hiring, training, benefits administration, compliance, and the setting of industry standards. What is the difference between today's unions performing an industry-wide function and the old guilds whose "purpose was to regulate, standardize and promulgate the different scales of wages and working conditions, to establish a traveling card system, to institute apprentice training and regulations on a standard basis and to acquaint local unions with the names of unworthy members who had to be disciplined or otherwise penalized . . ."

I shared a variation on the outsourcing concept at the PC Forum, an annual national meeting of high-tech entrepreneurs. My pitch was simple. Using data on outsourcing from McKinsey's Global Institute, I explained that if each company set aside 5 to 7 percent of the savings it achieved through its outsourcing of technology jobs, companies could create a pooled fund that would assist their dislocated workers in the transition to new employment. The fund could supplement dislocated workers' unemployment pay, bridge their health care for a defined period, and allow time for them to seek retraining and secure new employment. Similar funds thriving in SEIU's health care and building-service industries provide the proof of the viability of the idea. Intellectually, it was a straightforward argument that made solid business sense, but there were no takers among these high-tech entrepreneurs.

A New Organization for Contingent and Knowledge Workers—MyLife

AARP, the American Association of Retired Persons, with 35 million members, is a powerful organization in American society. AARP describes itself and its mission as follows:

AARP is a nonprofit, nonpartisan membership organization for people age 50 and over. AARP is dedicated to enhancing quality of life for all as we age. We lead positive social change and deliver value to members through information, advocacy and service.

Take out the "for people age 50 and over" and insert "American workers," and sign me up to create MyLife. MyLife would be a new organization whose purpose is to facilitate the ability of working Americans to manage their own work lives, especially the ever-expanding group of contingent and knowledge workers. As workers move from one employer to another or from self-employment to contracted employment, MyLife could advise, invest, and oversee workers' retirement funds. It could manage personal accounts, accept employers' defined contributions, and function just like TIAA-CREF or a universal 401(k) plan.

Imagine an organization representing millions of workers that could combine employer and employee contributions and offer lifetime health care benefits at lower costs. This new organization would have the advantage of large insurance pools, the key to lower health care costs. Additionally, it would be able to provide preventative care, one portable health record, and constant monitoring of individual physical conditions. Wouldn't it be progress if we never had to hear the terms *preexisting condition* or *COBRA* again? And, what if each person had only one set of medical records? What if we never again had to complete another medical history?

MyLife could post job openings, maintain résumés, track Social Security benefits, advise on educational opportunities, do wage comparisons, conduct financial counseling, and offer vacation and entertainment services while linking its members with other workers who did the same type of work so they could "talk shop." And, with millions of working Americans as members, MyLife could be a national voice on behalf of its members for reducing college costs, improving health care, reducing credit-card fees and interest rates, or reforming government policies on education and retraining. With your employer no longer the constant in your self-managed work life, why not a new permanent work partner?

Global Unions

The world needs global unions. Workers across the globe are frustrated with their inadequate emerging relationships with new multinational corporate employers. Individual workers certainly don't have the power to bargain effectively for themselves one work site at a time. National unions by their very nature are not built to have the strength to successfully address their members' issues when they operate in only one country of a global employer. Global unions would have the reach and strength to get the job done for workers everywhere.

In August 2005, one month after the dispiriting AFL-CIO Convention left town, the world's largest global union federation, Union Network International (UNI), with 15.5 million members from 900 unions and 140 countries, arrived in Chicago for its every-five-year meeting.

Under the banner "Imagine a Global Union," UNI delegates adopted a plan to begin a transition of its affiliates from a loose federation to a more integrated union, a concept that American unions had rejected several weeks earlier. The context for the debate over change in UNI had an eerily familiar ring with the discussion held a month earlier by AFL-CIO leaders. At their Chicago convention, UNI reported that they sought to enhance unions' impact worldwide: on their individual members, employers, and the public in general. They would continue to strive to let the world know that it was time for unions to adapt to a world without borders. UNI has organized its activities based on industry-sector groupings—the same structure we had proposed for the AFL-CIO that Change to Win had adopted.

In the late 1990s, SEIU's top leader in the Midwest, Tom Balanoff, had been elected chair of one of UNI's sectors, property services, a sector consisting of cleaning and security workers. The sector led a multiyear process with leaders from Sweden, Denmark, South America, and the Netherlands to push for far greater cooperation in our work with our multinational employers, and the work paid off. The sector launched a worldwide Justice for Janitors Day, commemorating the 1990 Los Angeles police riot.

Each year the UNI's Property Services Sector nominated employers to our "Top Trash List" of those who were denying workers their rights. UNI informed companies of their designation, which led some to settle. The other, more recalcitrant ones had their names publicized, and one "Top Trash" employer was chosen for worldwide protests.

UNI centered our coordination with global employers and our sector reached a first-ever worldwide agreement with Securitas, a high-quality, high-performance security contractor, and campaigned for rights of workers at Group 4 Securicor, an international security company headquartered in London with a US subsidiary Wackenhut. Our sector tested efforts that helped set the stage for UNI's debate on transformation.

With a mandate from SEIU's 2004 convention delegates to build a global union, followed by UNI's adoption of global unionism, SEIU assigned staff to Australia, Poland, England, India, France, Switzerland, Germany, the Netherlands, South America, and, soon, Africa. We sent teams of leaders to visit unions around the world to discuss new forms of alliances and relationships in many sectors, and we invested several million dollars in organizing campaigns that targeted international food-service, cleaning, and security employers.

SEIU is ramping up to operate on a global stage; we are learning the pitfalls and exploring the opportunities. We think about the new avenues opened up by global campaigns. For example, unions with strong financial assets working for the same multi-national employer can pay strike benefits to low-wage workers in countries with less-endowed unions who walk off their jobs. The opportunities are endless: Imagine simultaneous protests on service contractors' global clients, or outsourcing strikes to countries where strikes are legal and will not provoke government retaliation.

Until multinational corporations recognize the benefits of mutually beneficial partnerships with their employees, there are other tactical advantages of working globally. In the synchronized world of just-in-time arrangements, there are potential points for unions to hold companies accountable to their workers and communities which can have repercussions on their production timetables.

Further, employers now have a worldwide hiring hall, and global campaigns now have worldwide points of leverage. Global unions are in their infant stages, but several factors are helping them to mature more quickly than anyone would have imagined: the growing consolidation of corporations and the budding solidarity among unions within sectors, accelerated in part by employers resisting union relationships.

Global Social Responsibility and Responsible Competitiveness

What the future should hold is the convergence of global movements concerned with the environment, social responsibility, human rights, child labor, gender equality, and workers' rights. As companies now make the rules, these different advocacy movements will increasingly find themselves simultaneously trying to change the behavior of the same enterprises.

In South Africa during the apartheid era, advocacy organizations united their efforts by adopting the Sullivan Principles, a common set of demands to guide investment of corporations in the country. Corporate adherence to the principles of socially responsible investment was demanded by all parties seeking the establishment of a new South Africa. The McBride Principles, which would have penalized United States firms doing business in Northern Ireland unless they adhered to nondiscriminatory practices toward the Catholic minority, are another example of multiple advocates placing common demands for change on global companies.

The future global economy may see foundations, non-governmental organizations, unions, governments, and issue advocates uniting to tame the unruly nature of globalization with a common set of principles about responsible competitiveness, sustainable development, and fair employment practices, which become the vortex of a worldwide movement to make work pay for everyone.

CHAPTER SEVEN

Pushing Past Partisan Roadblocks

Unions have to undergo one final transformation in the way they operate to make them more effective advocates for working Americans and a vibrant force for facing the challenges of globalization in the twenty-first century: We have to modernize our methods of influencing the political process. John Sweeney's initiative at the AFL-CIO to create a highly effective political program was brilliant, but for a number of reasons, it could accomplish only so much. One, as the percentage of the workforce in unions decreased, we applied our talent to a smaller percentage of voters. Two, our members rightly saw us as too wedded to the Democratic establishment, a political party with no united agenda on worker issues. Three, our process for candidate endorsements was too insular. Four, our willingness to hold ourselves and elected officials accountable was inadequate.

Compounding these problems is the fact that our democracy is challenged by a decreasing citizen participation in our electoral process. Our country could choose to facilitate voting for all Americans rather than target or distort voting to the advantage of a candidate's or party's interest. There are a number of ways to increase participation: twenty-four-hour voting, election day as a national holiday, week-long voting, vote by mail, a tax credit for voting, mandatory voting like Australia, and same-day registration.

Candidates' increased addiction to money is another significant problem. I am in favor of "Clean Election" laws, which require candidates to raise a significant portion of their donations from small, individual donors. When the candidates reach a specified level, public funding becomes available, and any additional fund-raising is prohibited. At the presidential level, public financing is already in place and opting out should not be an option. Americans are right to be skeptical about their elected officials when billions of dollars of special-interest money, including labor money, flow into candidates' campaign treasuries and candidates spend much of their time raising money from the wealthy. While the system exists, we must live by it, but at the same time, we need to work to reform it.

In addition to supporting election reform, the labor movement has to embrace new ways of operating that are more democratic and incorporate their members' views of the candidates and their positions on the issues. Unions should be more engaged in formulating policy proposals to address areas of most urgent need, such as tax policy, health care, and retirement security, and they should use their clout to force those proposals onto the agenda of debate and hold politicians accountable for their promises.

THEY SHOULD WORK FOR US

In my position as president of SEIU, I have adopted a more independent non-partisan approach than that of my predecessors and have chosen not to serve in any official capacity in either party. Our members expect and deserve our decisions to be made only in their interests, independent from any party interests. Of the two parties, as a whole, the Democratic Party is by far the stronger supporter of issues that matter to the labor movement. It would be unfair not to disclose—and not believable to imagine otherwise—that my personal voting record is overwhelmingly Democratic. This is not to that say there are not individual Republicans whom I respect who have defied their party's orthodoxy on specific issues, such as Senator John McCain for his stance on immigration, former Illinois Governor George Ryan on the death penalty, and Governor Mitt Romney on health care reform. Given the common ground between issues of importance to SEIU and to the Democratic Party, it is not surprising that I have been more warmly welcomed into their fold; consequently, my thoughts are primarily directed their way.

Much of my concern with the Democratic Party echoes the thinking of Martin Luther King Jr.: "In the end we will remember not the words of our enemies, but the silence of our friends." On the whole, Democrats have left me frustrated with their weak and disparate voices about issues of work, and their failure to define themselves as a party that stands squarely on the side of American workers. Everyone knows what defines Republicans: free enterprise, a strong national defense, less regulation, smaller government, corporate interests, social conservatism, and individual responsibility. Can voters as easily define the Democratic Party's core beliefs?

The Democratic Party has failed to clearly establish what it stands for, who it is fighting for, and who it is standing up to. Perhaps even worse, it has allowed its image to be defined in the narrowest and most negative terms—by others. Democrats have let Republicans frame the economic debate—as one focused on the role of government and fewer taxes. In reality, the true economic debate should be focused on the needs, dreams, and aspirations of the vast majority of hardworking Americans.

National party conventions are both a staged performance to showcase the presidential nominees and a quadrennial gathering of the party's elite. Party conventions also reveal to even the most casual observers an enormous amount about the beliefs of the party that holds them. My 2004 Democratic Convention experience highlighted the party's troubles all too clearly. After the 2004 presidential election, Thomas Frank, author of *What's the Matter with Kansas?* described what has become a popular analysis of Democratic failure among working Americans in

2004. My shorthand version of Frank's thesis is that Democrats are perceived as latte-drinking, Volvo-driving, chardonnay-sipping, northeastern-, Harvard-, and Yale-educated liberals. My only dispute with his analysis rests on a single word: *perceived!*

The 2004 Democratic Convention—held in Boston, John Kerry's and Harvard's backyard—was too much of a showcase of why Democrats and not Kansans are the problem.

The opening-night reception for President Bill Clinton and Senator Hillary Clinton was being hosted by a powerful and wealthy Boston couple who owned a nursing home that SEIU had spent years trying to organize. According to a 2000 article in *Boston* magazine, the owner was quoted as saying, "Unions have no place, in my opinion, in the health care industry." Quite a point of view for the host of an important Democratic Party event. SEIU was finally able to organize one of his nursing homes, though the employees worked for five years without a contract. I would wager that the money spent on that opening night gala would have gone far in paying for those workers to gain the health care coverage they were seeking.

In the two years prior to the convention, SEIU had asked every Democratic candidate who we learned had accepted money from that family to return the donation. How could Democratic candidates seek our union's support and at the same time accept support from people who are avowedly opposed to their own employees' right to have a union? Some Democrats tried to offer the traditional response to our request to take sides in a strike: *It is risky and not appropriate for me to take sides in a labor-management dispute.* When we responded that it might be too risky for SEIU to take sides in their election, they began to understand our point of view. Candidates acceded to our request, sometimes reluctantly, but usually in a quite principled way, and either refused to accept or returned the money.

Prior to the convention, party leaders asked SEIU to give the nursing home owners "a pass" and allow them to host the important opening night's top-billed event. I was asked to keep my mouth shut for the good of Democratic unity.

This was not the first time I experienced the Democratic Party's preference for donors over workers at one of their national conventions. The 1988 convention was held in Atlanta, Georgia; and an early party for dignitaries was hosted at the home of builder and real estate owner John Portman, a renowned architect and developer whose creation of the Hyatt Regency and Atlanta Merchandise Mart shaped downtown Atlanta. For years, Portman had resisted janitors' efforts to unionize. SEIU wanted to picket his reception, what we considered a mild dose of shame. (We had considered dropping Ping-Pong balls with our Justice for Janitors slogan from a helicopter on the estate where the outdoor event was being held, or on the golf course where a fund-raising tournament was being played.) Democratic leaders brokered discussions with Portman's representatives and we left with hollow and vague promises to help resolve the janitors' dispute; those promises didn't survive the week. I heard Portman's party was great, though the workers are still poor.

Over the course of the 2004 convention week, I grew increasingly angered by omnipresent symbols of Thomas Frank's "perceptions." There were elite briefings for big donors — including union donors like me. Boston was awash in lavish parties in posh homes. The pampering of the skybox Democratic funders was to be expected, but the absence of a focus on workers was striking.

By contrast, I was impressed by the vitality of the first-ever Blogger's Ball. The bloggers' community seemed authentic and engaged. Many political analysts see them as the key to the future of elections by finding modern ways to connect people to the political process. In 2004, they were the unappreciated Internet voices of the Democratic Party — its young, digital future: Duncan Black of "Eschaton," Dave Johnson of "Seeing the Forest," Matthew Yglesias and Josh Marshall of "Talking

Points Memo," Eric Alterman of "Altercation," and Markos
Moulitsas Zúniga of "Daily Kos." They were on the cutting
edge of politics, interested in discussing what the party stood for,
but I noticed very few, if any, elite or big-name visitors at this
convention event. One of the biggest problems with the Democratic Party in recent years is that it has not connected effectively
enough with this powerful army in the field and harnessed
their energy and expertise in reaching out to educate and mobilize its base. Instead, the party has relied much too heavily on the
culture its leaders are most comfortable with—top-down organizing and fund-raising with big donors, which is one reason that
it has failed to produce a strong crop of presidential contenders
who know how to connect with those workers who have voted
Republican and who Thomas Frank is so perplexed by.

Over the years, I have become increasingly disgusted with
politics and politicians. Money, money, money seems to be the
topic of most calls I get from politicians. I grew so exasperated
by the requests in the buildup to the 2004 presidential election
that I responded to one congressman that I was in psycholog-
ical counseling to reconcile my identity crisis, asking him, *Was
I a leader of workers or an ATM machine?* The degree of disconnect between union membership and the party leadership
was driven home to me shortly after my election in 1996 as
SEIU president when I was invited along with a dozen or so
other donors to an infamous "Clinton coffee," where I had
the opportunity to talk with the president. I was starstruck
going to the White House, and I appreciated the opportunity,
but I came to learn that it was just routine donor care and
feeding. After too many of these events, I thought back to the
words I'd spoken when I accepted the SEIU presidency: Politicians are going to have to act like they're our friends and vote
like they're our friends, and not just talk like they're our friends.

For these reasons, I've encouraged an approach that focuses
less on the candidate's party affiliation or status as an incumbent
or challenger and more on where he or she stands on the issues

that matter to our members. I prefer a more bipartisan approach to SEIU's engagement in the political process. Our members are not interested in whether political candidates are labeled Democrats or Republicans or Left or Right; they are concerned with whether the candidates are right or wrong on the issues that matter in their lives.

After my election in 1996, I reached out to the Republican Party chair, Jim Nicholson, and SEIU became an "Eagle"—a $10,000 donor to the Republican National Committee. It was an expression of my interest in engaging Republicans on issues of concern to America's workers, and I was promised a conversation. The committee accepted SEIU's contribution but we never had our conversation. SEIU continues to keep an open mind and an open door: At the Republican Convention in 2000, we honored several Republican legislators. We also employ Republican advisers. In 2004, SEIU was actually the largest contributor to both the Democratic *and* the Republican Governors' Associations, a fact that confused both party establishments. Today, the Republican Party's agenda on issues of work is often not in our members' best interest. Yet, Democratic elected officials are not focused enough on the nexus of issues regarding making work pay. Republicans often write unions off, and, unfortunately, too often Democrats take us for granted. I empathize with our members' weariness with politics and politicians.

For the 2004 elections, SEIU's leadership created an unconventional and transparent, member-oriented process for candidates seeking our endorsement. We invited President Bush to participate in our process, though clearly SEIU members were not going to support him, given his positions on tax cuts for the wealthy, privatizing Social Security, and repealing worker-friendly executive orders. So we turned to the field of Democratic contenders to find a candidate.

SEIU felt strongly about shifting from the traditional mode of "checkbook politics" to one that was more oriented to our members and the issues they cared about. Our process began with leaders asking our members two questions: What were the issues that mattered most to them and what information did they need to effectively evaluate the candidates? In response, SEIU compiled voting records, asked each candidate to complete a written questionnaire, and videotaped interviews with the candidates on our members' priority issues. Profiles were created from this information and posted on our Web site for easy access. SEIU strongly urged candidates to visit our local unions and meet with members outside of Washington to provide a real-life exchange. We then took a presidential preference vote, in September 2003, at a meeting of fifteen hundred of our most active volunteers and top elected leaders.

As many critics have argued in the wake of John Kerry's loss in 2004, the Democratic establishment seems to prefer presidential nominees who were the smartest kids in their class, or at least come across that way. They favor nuanced policy experts who could make successful contestants on *Jeopardy!* or *College Bowl.* Republicans, on the other hand, have for many years preferred nominees who could have succeeded on *American Idol;* candidates who connect with average Americans and convey that they understand our concerns.

At SEIU we wanted to identify candidates who could pass what I call the "hang test." Before giving their traditional campaign stump speech, candidates were required to meet for an hour—without staff—with twenty-five SEIU members. We wanted to know if they could hang out comfortably with a social service worker, school aide, or janitor, or have lunch at a diner or a beer in a neighborhood bar.

The Democratic Party leadership must develop a better tuning fork for these qualities in its candidates. Voter mobilization, money, strategy, and a grasp of the issues can get a candidate 80 percent of the way to victory, but *who that person is*—the person's ability to convey authenticity, humanity, and core values—adds the 20 percent that the candidate must contribute on his or her own.

SEIU's member interview—our "hang test"—was a process to judge candidates' ability to connect with real voters, and, as a portent of the election-night results revealed months later, it was quite effective: The eventual Democratic nominee, John Kerry, did not excel in our test.

When we outlined our elaborate process to the candidates, their campaign managers thought we were crazy. I sensed their disbelief that, unlike most other unions, where the president essentially makes the endorsement with a small group of top leaders, our members had a huge role. Many presumed that a direct appeal to me would be an effective shortcut. On each occasion, I reinforced our process, provided candidates with a list of our Executive Board, and encouraged them to meet with our local unions and members around the country.

The only candidate who got it was Governor Dean—and he did it. He came to countless picket lines and membership meetings, and spent so much time on the phone with our leaders that I began to wonder which presidency he was seeking—the United States' or SEIU's. Toward the end of the primary season, Senator John Edwards, realizing the help he could gain from SEIU members, spent increasing amounts of time with them. Other candidates continued to ignore our members and tried to romance me directly.

In the end, Dean won the preference poll of a field of nine candidates with over 50 percent, with John Edwards coming in second. Dean was the only outsider candidate, and he was boldly challenging the system. Not surprisingly, our janitors and health care workers felt a special kinship with him. Dean's honesty, unapologetic focus on repairing the country's health care system, unabashed willingness to say the word *union* in nonunion settings, and his public support for nurses who were organizing a union in his home state contributed to his success with SEIU members.

Ultimately, SEIU was joined by AFSCME, the second-largest union in the AFL-CIO, and by the Painters Union in

endorsing Dean, which was a blockbuster triple-crown for
Dean and created a roadblock for U.S. Representative Dick
Gephardt's hope of a primary victory fueled by the AFL-CIO's
endorsement. Representative Gephardt was a devoted, longtime
ally of the labor movement, but without the support of our three
large unions, he no longer could garner the two-thirds vote
required for an endorsement. Dick had led the fight against bad
trade agreements, and his long-standing support for unions, and
his personal decency, made conveying SEIU's decision an
unpleasant personal moment for me, but the process had
selected Dean as our recommended candidate. Democracy can
produce unexpected results.

Of course, hindsight gives perfect vision, and the endorsement of Dean at this point looks to many critics like a miscalculation, but it was not one to our members. Needless to say, the
Dean endorsement decision was not warmly received in the
house of labor or among Washington insiders, who thought he
was unelectable and uncontrollable. His infamous overexuber-
ance at the result of the Iowa caucus certainly turned the tide
against him by giving that impression. But the overriding issue
that should not be forgotten is that the other candidates had simply failed to make a persuasive case to our membership. Our
members wanted an honest candidate with clear positions on
issues of concern to them who would govern with a respect for
American families and sensitivity for the challenges they face and
whom they trusted to stick to his promises once elected. Dean
was the only one who convinced them that he had those qualities. They lacked the crystal ball available to the Democratic
insiders who so confidently predicted Al Gore's and John
Kerry's victories.

For me, this was another of what I've come to call my
"Cassie moments," when my daughter's courage gives me
resolve. The courage to do what was right, in this case for our
members, outweighed my concerns about upsetting the Democratic political establishment or my colleagues in the labor

movement. When the tide turned against Dean after Iowa, SEIU and the Painters stayed on deck until the bitter end; our members are not fair-weather friends, and we felt that the governor deserved to end his campaign by his choice or the voters', not by the desertion of his crew. When Kerry won the nomination, we threw our support behind him with full force.

The degree of SEIU's commitment to Kerry was questioned during the campaign because of an article in *The Washington Post* that reported on a meeting I had with members of the editorial staff. I had expected only the editorial board at that meeting, but they had invited columnists and political writers as well, including David Broder, the dean of American political writers. I spent an hour with the *Post* discussing a range of issues, many relating to the need for change in the labor movement and the Democratic Party.

I was asked if it would be easier or harder to change the AFL-CIO and the Democratic Party if John Kerry won the presidency. I answered, *Harder.* I elaborated that for labor and Democratic party leaders a Kerry victory meant White House dinners, movies with the President, bill signings, access to cabinet secretaries, and consultations with White House staff. We erroneously would think labor was going to be "saved" by the new administration and the party would become the captive of a new president. Then I added, "But that doesn't mean I don't want John Kerry to win." Columnist and reporter David Broder returned to the question several times, and I repeated my answer, until our last exchange, when I unfortunately omitted my caveat that it "doesn't mean I don't want John Kerry to win." I was unaware that my small mistake was going to become grist for a bigger story.

I was shocked to learn that evening, after reading David Broder's on-line story, that I was going to be tomorrow's news. *The Washington Post*'s story, under the headline "SEIU CHIEF SAYS THE DEMOCRATS LACK FRESH IDEAS; STERN ASSERTS THAT A KERRY WIN COULD SET BACK EFFORTS TO REFORM THE PARTY," reported that I wanted Kerry to lose the election because it would be easier for me to win the changes I felt were needed in the labor movement and the party, a distortion of the point I'd actually argued.

The story created quite a stir, and even my most loyal friends wondered if I had lost my mind. I spent that night and the next day "walking the story back." John Kerry and his staff, no strangers to media gaffes, were gracious. But a few of my colleagues in the labor movement publicly questioned my judgment and commitment. They happily disregarded the evidence to the contrary: the $65 million SEIU was spending in the elections, our help creating two new organizations to increase voter participation, and the thousands of SEIU Members working throughout the battleground states. Lesson learned: Beware of the distortions of even the best of our media coverage, and never underestimate its power to persuade.

Mobilizing the Forces

The more important story about SEIU's involvement in the campaign is about our grassroots mobilizing work. Our 2004 primary-election efforts were not focused solely on candidates. Addressing the nation's health care crisis was at the top of our members' agenda, and we undertook a nonpartisan campaign to stimulate debate around America's eroding health care system, hoping to elevate health care to the top of voters' agenda as well. Nurses from Iowa and New Hampshire were the faces of this SEIU effort. In SEIU's first issue ads of the primary season, the nurses filled television and radio airwaves and airport billboards with the message: "Running for President? Health Care Better Be your Priority."

Our members, wearing their purple SEIU shirts, attended every possible candidate event and challenged candidates about where they stood on health care until each developed a comprehensive plan. Candidates, accustomed to seeing purple-clad SEIU members at their events, would answer our members' health care questions before they were even asked. These were SEIU's best efforts to infuse the primaries with issues important to Americans, and it worked. In 2004, I attended Iowa Governor Tom Vilsack's health care forum, where every candidate acknowledged our nurses and told stories of their constant presence, explaining their by-then very well-developed health care plans.

SEIU also helped found and fund two new important organizations. The seeds for these organizations were planted by two of the progressive movement's smartest political strategists, Gina Glantz, one of the first campaign managers ever to use computer technology to communicate with and track voters in 1974 and former campaign manager for Senator Bill Bradley's presidential run in 2000, and Steve Rosenthal, whose work experiences range from senior positions with the Communications Workers of America, the Democratic National Committee, the U.S. Department of Labor under President Clinton, and the AFL-CIO's Committee on Political Education (COPE).

Gina and Steve had lived through the failed efforts of previous Democratic attempts to coordinate their activities and envied the Republican Party's ability to keep its constituency groups working together. Gina, Steve, and others, including Ellen Malcolm, the visionary founder of EMILY's List, Carl Pope, the executive director of the Sierra Club, Harold Ickes, a former Clinton aide, Cecile Richards, a long-time political organizer, and I founded America Coming Together (ACT). ACT was a 527 political committee dedicated to mobilizing voters to participate in the 2004 election. It was supported by many funders, most notably philanthropist George Soros, and Peter Lewis, the former CEO of the Progressive Insurance Company. America Votes, the other organization SEIU helped create, was a coalition of many large-membership organizations whose goal was to increase voter registration, education, and participation in the 2004 elections; it has survived the election cycle and is growing to become an even more important grass-roots effort.

By 2003, SEIU's Political Action Committee, funded by members' small, voluntary contributions, was the largest labor PAC, and the second largest of all PACs in the country. SEIU had record-setting plans for 2004 of involving and mobilizing our members like never before: a signature strategy, which we ultimately achieved, of recruiting and mobilizing 2004 full-time campaign workers—"Heroes," who worked from three to six months full-time registering, educating, and mobilizing voters. We also mobilized 50,000 part-time volunteers to be the infrastructure for this massive effort. Ultimately, SEIU spent the unprecedented sum of $65 million to help mobilize working families in the 2004 presidential election cycle.

In addition to this staggering display of people power, SEIU had four mobile action centers—technologically retrofitted, traveling tractor-trailer phone centers, which conveniently brought the phones to volunteers, rather than making volunteers come to them; these traveling phone centers, along with SEIU's more traditional call centers, gave us the capacity to make thousands of calls to voters per hour. Our phone banks, our army of volunteers, and our political contributions combined to make SEIU a force to be reckoned with in the presidential primary process.

All of these efforts helped produce the largest turnout of progressive voters in history. Turnout wasn't quite enough to defeat President Bush, but rather than consider the efforts a bust, as some critics have in the wake of the election, I believe in building on the foundation of what we have accomplished as we head into the next election.

If the Democratic Party wants to win elections, it needs a permanent infrastructure that is not controlled by the party's elected officials and that employs and integrates the modern techniques of data management, marketing, mobilizing, and new communication technologies. It also need a message that is compelling to voters. Bill Clinton's two victories were not due to a Democratic Party infrastructure but were the result of his self-assembled, highly talented campaign staff and consultants, his finely honed, disciplined message that directly addressed issues of concern to voters, and his extraordinary charisma and leadership. The Republican Party has built an efficient electoral machine and the Democrats are constantly reinventing theirs. Democrats have failed to build a stable state-by-state electoral infrastructure and only recently developed a small donor fundraising program to support its nominees. Despite endless meetings on "message" and countless polls, there is not yet the desire on the part of Democratic elected officials to speak with one voice on issues important to hardworking Americans, particularly on how their work is going to be valued.

If the Democratic Party wants to win back those "perplexing" working Americans who, Thomas Frank argues, are voting against their own interests, it's going to have to start connecting much more effectively with working Americans. Consider this one simple but powerful story about just how out of touch the party leadership was the last time around.

As the 2004 Democratic Convention headed to its dramatic climax—the nominee's acceptance speech—Senator Kerry was empowered with a critically important moment in which to introduce and define himself to the electorate. Every aspect of that night was staged with exacting precision. Where to enter? Who was on the podium? How long to speak to ensure maximum news exposure? What color tie? And who would get the premier placement with the Kerry family in their private box?

As has become custom in the State of the Union and other important addresses, the choice of who is honored to take these prime seats at key events is highly symbolic. For the State of the Union, presidents often choose lifesaving firefighters, teachers from urban schools, or returning soldiers. The possibilities are endless, but the choice is strategic. And, it is not a choice that goes unnoticed by the commentators and pundits who report on and parse the selection with great nuance.

When I saw who Kerry had chosen to seat next to his wife on the night that he introduced himself to the voters, I was dismayed. Having opened his address with, "I'm John Kerry, and I'm reporting for duty," Senator Kerry had an opportunity to communicate that his duty was to those Americans who were apprehensive about their economic future and who could *not* afford an invitation to the exclusive parties. But he didn't. The seat of honor next to Teresa Heinz was reserved for Robert Rubin, former hero of Wall Street and Clinton's treasury secretary. Now don't get me wrong: I think Bob Rubin was a solid steward of our economy, despite his overstated views on the value of trade. Who would begrudge him the best seat in the house? But Kerry's choice of a corporate CEO and Wall Street adviser, rather than a small businessman or nurse from Kansas, is part of the answer to the oft-asked question of why workers seem to "vote against their interests."

Dead Armadillos

As former Texas Agriculture Commissioner Jim Hightower once said, "There's nothing in the middle of the road but yellow stripes and dead armadillos." The Democratic Party cannot continue to sit in the middle of the road on trade, wage inequality, corporate responsibility, fair taxes, and unions and win elections. The Republicans are not confused. They made their choice a long time ago. Republicans' trickle-down economics and tax policies favor the wealthy and everyone knows it. The Bush-Cheney governing philosophy puts big business at the head of the table. Lobbyist Jack Abramoff and former Majority Leader Tom DeLay greased palms and disciplined the wayward; they are gone, but unquestionably someone will take their place. Big corporations and K Street lobbyists feed at the same trough.

But the Democratic Party is stymied. Will it protect the interests of Main Street or Wall Street? Will it fight for the electrician or the elite? The outsiders or the owners? The Democratic Party's fear of getting caught in an economic crossfire between its base and its financially endowed allies, I believe, traps them in a perpetually losing posture. As former New York Governor Mario Cuomo once observed of the traditional Democratic working-class voter way back in 1974: "They were the backbone of our party . . . Then we lost them. For some reason they felt alienated by a new Democratic Party which they thought neither understood nor related to them. They were made to feel voiceless, powerless and frustrated. . . . We must bring them back to our party. Without them, we can neither win nor regard ourselves as entitled to win." Three decades after Cuomo's observation, the Democratic Party is still fighting over their identity when they should be generating policies that value hard work.

The Democratic Party can try to mediate its way between the conflicting economic interests of its constituencies, but they can't have it both ways and win elections. Democrats need to wake up every day infused with passion to govern for those who work hard and play by the rules.

Unfortunately, the Democratic Party is best known for what it stands against—Republicans. They should stop the Bush bashing and talk about the nation's problems. They need to become the party of ideas, solutions, and the future. The answer to every question is not the protection of the old, nor is it a new government program. In order to recapture the middle-class, middle-aged, middle American voters who often "vote against" their economic self-interest, Democrats need to offer an alternative economic agenda that is built around the realities and promise of the twenty-first-century global economy. The agenda should contain clear, simple principles that appeal to voters' common sense.

Republicans need to understand that rewarding work is a

moral, spiritual, and religious value; greed is not. They should stop bashing liberals and focus less on making K Street lobbyists rich than on making ordinary Americans better off. The ownership society can't work if people only own debt. And those that accept personal responsibility shouldn't work every day and be poor. Workers' choice to join a union should hold equal value with other choices that Republicans champion—schools, guns, and religion.

Our entire nation would be better off if both parties' candidates would run for office on their own clear values, not poll- and focus-group–tested messages. Americans want progress. They seek opportunity and accept responsibility. Most know that our country is very different today from when they started to work, and that even more change is on the way. Americans are looking for true leadership, honest discourse, and solutions, not excuses.

Change in neither party will come about easily, which is why unions must become an even more effective force for change. One important way to fight for change is to hold elected officials accountable for their campaign promises. SEIU has helped to form a new organization to do just that. They Work for Us will shine a light on the records of incumbent Democrats who fail to show a true commitment to populist economic policies, including supporting increasing the minimum wage, a plan to improve our health care system, and a commitment to workers' rights to organize.

The political process has become so polarized that neither party is effectively addressing the crucial issues confronting the majority of Americans. It is time—in fact, it is long overdue—for both parties to rise above partisan politics and focus on working Americans and the issues that matter to them and their kids' future.

CHAPTER EIGHT

Don't Let Them Fool You

America is another "mass institution" that needs a plan for change. The reality of our times is that mind work dominates muscle work—whether you are a UPS driver, a sheet metal worker, or a nurse's aide. Government needs to guide change. Its role is to supply direction and advice, offer the right incentives, ensure a safety net for the vulnerable, and provide financial resources, physical infrastructure, and investment in human capital. The answer to every problem is not a new government program or regulation. Nor can we continue to recite old answers for new realities.

THE DIVERSIONS

The road to creating a country that works for all of us is littered with stale ideas, competing theories, and misinformation that divert us from real solutions. Politicians and business leaders who benefit from the status quo have incentives to paint rosy pictures and extol the virtues of the American economy. After all, the economy is growing. Trade is booming. High-tech jobs are waiting in the wings. And, last but definitely not least, education—*what you learn is what you earn*—is a ready answer to all working families.

So, why worry? Let's just do more of the same: implement more tax cuts for businesses and the wealthy and continue to

underfund public education. Give more flexibility to employers; remove regulations preventing pollution, or drilling for
oil on federal land; stop trial lawyers from getting restitution
for workers killed by corporate negligence; and keep workers
from having rights at work. Somehow, working families will be
okay. As a *New York Times* headline pronounced several years
ago: "LOOKS LIKE A RECOVERY, FEELS LIKE A RECESSION."
Let's take a closer look at some of the diversions that prevent us
from creating an economy that produces broad-based growth.

The Growing-Economy Diversion

When expressing concern for the American economy, I am
often asked: But isn't the economy growing? Yes, I answer,
but let's not forget that growth is not the same as producing
equitable distribution.

It is true that America has been blessed with healthy overall
economic growth, increased productivity, and record corporate
profits. No question, growth is good. But growth and productivity do not automatically guarantee that the gains will be
divided fairly.

In the boom period following World War II, growth, productivity, profits, and wages were closely related, rising and
falling together. But since 1979, growth, productivity, profits,
and executive compensation have all skyrocketed, while most
workers' wages have stagnated.

- Between 1980 and 2004, productivity increased 68 percent
  but the wages of the average production worker barely
  budged. On the other hand, the total value of the stock market rose 793 percent and CEO pay rose 743 percent.
- A recent survey of two hundred large companies reported
  that in 2005 the average annual pay for a CEO—$11.3
  million—increased 27 percent over the preceding year, while

the average worker's income — $43,480 — rose only 2.9 percent, below the 3.3 percent inflation rate.

This economy has unhinged the relationship between growth, productivity, and wages. As Harvard economist Benjamin Friedman said, "Broad-based economic growth in America was not a myth. . . . A rising standard of living for the great majority of our citizens has in fact been the American norm, and it is we, today, who are failing to achieve it." Although theories abound about the failure of the economy to distribute equitable results due to a lack of infrastructure investment or fiscal discipline, the reality is that American workers' wage increases have been cut loose from growth, productivity, and profits.

As the 1992 Clinton campaign's War Room proclamation — "It's the economy, stupid" — was a rallying call for America at the end of the twentieth century, "It's income inequality, stupid" must be the uniting call at the dawning of a new century.

The Average-Wage Diversion

Politicians and some economists like to point to the increase in "average" wages as evidence of a just and fair economy. True, average wages are up, but you do not need an MBA from Harvard to understand that the increase in the average wage is due to those at the top of the economic ladder, who have seen their wages rise by astonishing amounts — even as the wages of 90 percent of Americans grew by a paltry amount:

- Between 1972 and 2001, the income of Americans at the 90th percentile rose 34 percent; those with income in the 99th percentile rose 181 percent; those with income in the 99.9th percentile rose 497 percent. By contrast, the median American family saw its income rise by a mere 26 percent over the same thirty years — less than 1 percent per year.

The *New York Times* columnist and economist Paul Krugman discussed the fallacy of the average-wage theory in a recent column. The problem can be illustrated by this example: If three nurses are sitting in a break room during their shift and the first nurse earns $80,000 per year and the other two nurses each earn $50,000 per year, the average wage is $60,000. When the $80,000 nurse leaves to answer a patient call, and Ray Irani, CEO of Occidental Petroleum, becomes the third person in the room, the average wage becomes $21,333,000. No nurse got a raise, but average wages skyrocket as Irani's $63 million of total compensation is included in the calculations.

As our example shows, the increase in average wages masks the true economic picture for the majority of Americans. The distribution of wages in the United States is now more highly skewed, meaning that a smaller share of workers earn extremely high wages, while the bulk of the workers earn much less, but the top wage earners raise the average. The median wage tells you the precise middle of the income distribution—half of wage earners make more, half earn less—so, in the case of skewed distribution, it gives a more accurate picture of the "typical" worker. Real median household income has fallen every year since 1999 and was 4 percent lower in 2004 than it was in 1999. So the rich got richer, the poor got poorer, and the middle got squeezed down year after year. When politicians are touting average-wage figures, it is most likely an intentional misdirection to mask the true reality of today's economy.

The Market Diversion

Many in the business and political elite have tried to sell the public the "market elixir" miracle cure for all our economic problems. An unencumbered free market, they say, distributes wealth naturally. As the previous statistics dramatize, if we consume any more of the market elixir, America's cities, from Miami Beach, to

Kansas City, to Los Angeles, will begin to feel like São Paulo, Brazil, where the rich helicopter from building to building in order to avoid the devastating poverty on the streets below. As Robert Shapiro, a noted economist from the Clinton administration, said in a May 2006 meeting of the NDN, formerly known as the New Democrat Network, the old rules of the market are just not working to raise wages for most Americans.

China's emerging elite has swallowed the elixir, and their new reliance on the market has resulted in the greatest disparity of wealth in the world. Elected leaders of many South American countries are rejecting the World Bank/IMF market-based initiatives. Reducing the role of government in the economy by ending restrictions and regulations on business and promoting privatization of public assets to "open" the market have exacerbated rather than solved the distribution problem. According to the *Toronto Globe and Mail*:

> During the past twenty years, many Latin nations have implemented International Monetary Fund–prescribed reforms designed to open markets, tighten budgets, and privatize services, only to see economic growth slow down. Meanwhile, the continent's income disparity, already the world's largest, has widened and millions of people have become poor. Today, more than one-third of South Americans live in poverty and, in many countries, the richest 10 percent control more than half of all income.

To expect the "free market" to be the force to justly reward American workers is simply off base.

The Trade Diversion

America has pushed through trade agreements to open its markets ever since NAFTA was sold to the public as a job-creating, wage-lifting boon to the American economy. The United States helped negotiate China's entrance into the World Trade Organization, and now trade agreements roll on across the globe. Many of these agreements provoked fierce legislative battles resulting in deep scars and mistrust between the union movement and the Democratic Party leadership that made the case for NAFTA, and frustrated and angered many working Americans in states hardest hit by job loss.

The fact is that free trade has not been fair trade.

Because I'm a union leader, some caveats are in order. I am not arguing that we should revert to protectionism. The cat is out of the bag, particularly since China entered the global market. While skeptical, I *might* accept that macroeconomically free trade has benefited the American economy. The problem is that the benefits have not alleviated the severe hit that good-paying jobs have taken, first in manufacturing and now in white-collar sectors. When the jobs leaving the country pay significantly more than the jobs being created, any rational family facing that steep economic adjustment downward would fight to stop what they perceive as the enemy.

Living with the fallout every day, many Americans view trade as a threat to their families and to their children's future. Some business leaders say that this response is irrational, but the CEOs and other beneficiaries of free trade are not convincing Americans of its benefits. As Gene Sperling, Senior Fellow at the Center for American Progress and former national economic adviser to President Clinton, wrote in his book *The Pro-Growth Progressive*: " . . . those who argue against protectionism often have nothing to say to those facing pain and devastation today but 'tough luck.' This leads to an impoverished impasse: when it comes to workers and communities threatened by global competition, protectionists have no vision for the future and free traders have no vision for the present." What *is* irrational is our business and political leaders' indifference to finding ways to create good American jobs as replacements. Trade has become the hot button for the debate over the economic divide. Parents with children to raise will appropriately fight trade policies that hurt them by sending their good-paying jobs overseas and replacing them with jobs with lower wages and reduced benefits.

Until the jobs being created in the economy and the existing 50 million hard-to-export service-sector jobs—in transportation, logistics, retail, health care, food processing, and hospitality—pay enough for you to own a home and raise a family, the debate over trade will continue to boil.

The High-Tech Job Diversion

Jobs in the high-tech industry were acclaimed not long ago as the bridge to the twenty-first century, but that calculation missed two now-apparent trends.

Digitization made possible the transfer of white-collar work to anywhere in the world at the touch of a button, and for far less cost.

- American companies lead the world in offshoring *white-collar* jobs to low-wage countries. Today they employ more than 900,000 offshore service workers doing everything from developing software to answering customers' questions and conducting research and development. By 2008, U.S. companies are expected to employ more than 2.3 million offshore service workers.
- For the cost of one engineer in the United States, a company can hire eleven in India. In 2005, Indian engineers earned an average salary of $9,559, drawing even more American and European white-collar jobs offshore.
- China and India, particularly, and now developing countries as well, boast a huge talent pool. In 2003, China had 9.6 million professional graduates with up to seven years of work experience. India's supply of young professionals is approx-

imately 14 million. High-tech jobs no longer look likely to replace the middle-class jobs of the industrial economy that were lost in droves as manufacturing moved overseas.

The All-Purpose-Education Diversion

Finally, the most frequently voiced answer to America's economic problems is: *Get an education.* Many liberals and conservatives honestly believe that education is the answer to distributing wealth more equitably. I think they are wrong.

I do believe strongly in education and the power and value of learning. For SEIU's members, particularly immigrants, their children's education is a passion, and I respect that enormously. The opportunity for a high-quality education is, of course, essential to equality and social mobility. Training in appropriate skills is critical for preparing the workforce we need in the future. College should be available and affordable for all Americans who have the desire and capacity to improve themselves.

But, but, but—education is not going to solve the distribution dilemma for our society as a whole.

The "Education Is the Answer" mantra has problems. The faster the pace of economic change, the more difficult the accuracy of projecting future skill and education requirements. I don't think anyone could have predicted the results of a recent study demonstrating that today it's the more *highly skilled* service-sector jobs most likely to be offshored.

Most important, if we look to tomorrow's world of work, that snapshot of the future does not predict a boom for college graduates in either job opportunities or pay.

- The proportion of jobs that require a college degree is expected to rise by *only 1 percent,* from 26.9 in 2002 to 27.9 in 2012. Only eight of the thirty fastest-growing jobs will require a college degree. The 2006 Economic Report of the

President shows that between 2000 and 2004, the real earnings of college graduates *fell* more than 5 percent.

Given those facts, policies premised only on the value of getting an education are inadequate.

In fact, there is good data to show that our system of higher education—rather than promoting equal opportunity—is aggravating the economic divide. In the hundred-yard college dash, the most advantaged Americans are starting on the fifty-yard line.

- In 2003, at the most prestigious private universities, more freshmen had fathers who were doctors than clergy, teachers, hourly workers, and members of the military combined.
- In the top 146 colleges, three out of one hundred students— only 3 percent—are from the bottom quartile of income.
- According to the U.S. Congress Advisory Committee on Student Financial Assistance, the high price of an education has prevented almost half of qualified high-school graduates from matriculating at four-year colleges, and one out of five from attending any college at all.
- Since 1981, the cost of a four-year private college has risen by 202 percent, while the Consumer Price Index has risen only 80 percent.

Universal public education is a hallmark of American democracy—one of our great achievements—but claims that education alone is the remedy for America's economic ills or the mechanism to distribute wealth more fairly is pabulum for the chattering classes.

A NEW WAY TO MEASURE

In order to move beyond the substantive diversions that inhibit a more rational and fair discussion of public needs, political leaders and policy makers must first get serious about creating better measurements for analysis. Empirical evidence and data drive everything in today's economy from corporate strategies and investment decisions to government budgets and union negotiations with employers. Unfortunately, many of the economic indicators we use to guide these decisions are as outdated and irrelevant to workers' lives as the industrial and manufacturing era in which they were created. Consequently, the magnitude of pressures facing middle-class families goes unnoticed, and public discourse about what families really need to get ahead and build a stable life remains misguided.

In a rational world, Americans would turn on the evening news to get information about how many paychecks the average family was away from falling into unmanageable debt or how many families were at risk of bankruptcy due to medical emergencies. Families could use these and other commonsense indicators to assess the overall strength of the economy and their own economic positions. Politicians in turn would use these measures to make decisions that could alleviate risk and provide greater opportunity, such as reductions in payroll taxes, universal health care coverage, or new pools for catastrophic-risk insurance.

But we do not live in a rational world. Americans turn on the news to find pundits, politicians, and administration officials talk up the wonders of an economy with marginal percentage increases in growth, slightly higher average wages from one year ago, and reports about the Dow Jones and NASDAQ indicators closing higher for the month. Families hear the good news but wonder why they have missed out. With scant regard for the disconnect of many of these indicators to people's lives, our political leaders use these trends as justifications for permanent tax reductions for the wealthy and the shifting of health care, education, and retirement burdens onto the backs of individuals. Anyone who criticizes these policies is considered a purveyor of "class warfare."

Instead of data that enlightens our political leaders and creates more sensible public-policy discussions, our current indicators mask important trends and obscure what could be fairly straightforward and achievable options for increasing the financial status of 90 percent of American families.

The missing ingredient in modern economics is clear: We need solid measures of economic security and opportunity rather than more finely sliced data on economic output or macroeconomic trends. GDP, job growth, unemployment, productivity, inflation, average home sales, graduation rates, stock indexes, and other measures are important, but collectively they tell us little about the real economic state of working families. According to analysts at the Center for American Progress, meaningful measures of economic security would take into account:

1. Not just how much income the average household makes, but median income.
2. Not just job growth, but the rate of pay and the stability of the jobs being created.
3. Not just interest rates, but how much debt families are carrying just to pay for the basic costs of life.
4. Not just how many people own homes or the median value of these homes, but how many people have been able to build real equity in the homes they own.
5. Not just the number of people who have health insurance (although that number is very important on its own), but how much health care costs have risen in recent years—and how much of those costs families have to bear.
6. Not just the rate of inflation, but how much the basic costs of life are rising for middle-class families, including housing, food, transportation, college education, medical expenses, etc.
7. Not just stock ownership percentages or 401(k) enrollment rates, but the overall amount of income families have at their disposal to invest in these wealth-building opportunities.

The factors that determine economic security and opportunity are straightforward; we just need to be more creative and persistent in collecting and analyzing them. Just as the saber-metrics revolution has taken off in baseball to provide a richer understanding of the real contributions of players to teams, we need to unleash our leading economic analysts to measure more useful, relevant statistics and create a more satisfying public debate about our collective future.

To meaningfully analyze how much risk families are bearing, we need to know some basic facts:

- Could the average family survive a medical emergency without going into bankruptcy? By what margin?
- How many paychecks away from bankruptcy is the average American family?
- How many families could survive the lost income of a laid-off family member if they had to wait the average of 20 weeks it takes to find a new job?
- How many weeks of economic cushion does the average family have before it would have to declare bankruptcy? How many families have 6 months, or a year's worth of cushion?

With these and other facts in hand, our decision makers would be better equipped and informed of the real status of their constituents. Corporate leaders would be more aware of the consequences of rapacious business practices that rush to the bottom on wages and benefits. Union leaders would be stronger advocates for their members. And Americans across the board would have a keener understanding of where they actually stand in life and what they need to do—and demand from leaders—to live out the American Dream.

Toward a Country That Works

We might consider taking a trip backward in time—to the early 1970s, when Americans, even those with little education, were rewarded fairly and the rewards of success were better distributed. Everyone was better off for it. The industrial economy employed many unskilled workers with only high-school degrees. They turned bolts on assembly lines, mined coal with pickaxes, and threw ore into blast furnaces. But these were jobs that raised families, allowed for home ownership, had health care coverage, helped send kids to college, and protected the American Dream.

Fair pay didn't come to fruition by the generosity of factory owners or solely by the mechanisms of the free market. Fair pay had to be fought for within industries by unions and politically through government.

When today's janitors, health and home care workers, truck drivers, retail workers, and construction laborers can earn enough to live their lives as easily as their counterparts of the industrial era, then America will be a better country again. That is the proper standard—the American standard—we should set to evaluate our progress going forward.

With a serious, ambitious plan, America could stride boldly into the future. Without one, America will merely stagger forward and will eventually fall behind. Hardworking Americans are paying too high a price for their leaders' failures to tackle challenges that are surmountable.

We can create a country we can all be proud of—an America where dreams still come true. But we must be honest as a nation about our changing environment, avoid diversions, and come together with a plan. America's future is not a matter of chance—it's a matter of choice.

CHAPTER NINE

A Plan for a Country That Works

No one can predict how, at any particular moment in history, change will happen. Life would be easier if there were a road map or a proven mathematical formula that would lay out how to get from point A, to point B, to point C. Yet, life rarely works out that way. Neither does the change process. As I looked hard at the growing problems facing the country, I realized that I, like many Americans, had been waiting for the most conventional solution: a president or visionary new leader to take hold of the tiller and sail America on a new course. And then it struck me—if there is no wind, even with the finest leader at the helm, the boat will just slowly drift in the current. It is the wind that fills the sails and makes the boat move through our troubled waters, hopefully steered on a safe course by our leaders' steady hands.

I grew up in an era when the winds of change were gusting.

The civil rights movement was led by courageous women like Rosa Parks and nonviolent, principled leaders like Martin Luther King Jr. and John Lewis, who stood their ground on the Edmund Pettus Bridge outside Selma. The women's movement was inspired by the writings of Betty Friedan and Gloria Steinem and led millions of women to reexamine their lives as mothers, daughters, wives, and citizens. Denis Hayes launched Earth Day, a movement calling on America to respect and preserve our environment. A consumer movement led by a young lawyer named Ralph Nader brought about impressive improvements in product safety. The antiwar movement marched on Washington and lost lives at Kent State, energizing and politicizing hundreds of thousands of students and launching Senator Eugene McCarthy's presidential bid.

Each of these movements, sparked by different seminal events, was founded by and energized by the actions of "ordinary" Americans who were the winds of change, not sponsored by professional politicians or lobbied for by K Street suits. I often say to my colleagues, including friends in the media and in Congress, that change has been the product of Americans' raising their voices in living rooms and protesting on the streets. At best, those colleagues regard me as naïve and unsophisticated for not accepting Washington's supreme role as the center for all thought and progress. Even Napoleon Bonaparte recognized the power of people: "Men who have changed the world never achieved their success by winning the chief citizens to their sides, but always by stirring the masses."

The Beltway's revisionist history often disregards the big forces of change that came from outside Washington, such as those of my youth in the sixties and seventies that led to the twentieth century's great legislative breakthroughs in civil, consumer, and women's rights. Martin Luther King didn't pen the "Letter from a Birmingham Jail" in a fancy downtown Washington restaurant. Ralph Nader may have resided in Washington, but he came to prominence by taking on Detroit's auto behemoths that built cars "unsafe at any speed." Betty Friedan and Gloria Steinem and Dolores Huerta fought for women's rights at home and in the workplace, whether in the fields of Salinas or the skyscrapers of Fifth Avenue. The students who fought for free speech at Berkeley or against the Vietnam War at Kent State didn't turn to Washington to set their agendas.

Who doubts that when a half-million immigrants and native-born protesters took to the streets of Los Angeles, followed by millions more from small towns and big cities, the 2006 immigration debate was reenergized and reframed? Indeed, we may be witnessing the birth of the first new mass movement of the twenty-first century.

Or consider the power of protest when millions of French students, unionists, and citizens participated in the 2006 general strikes in opposition to legislation to roll back employment protections for young workers. The protests brought to mind Paris in 1968 and shook French lawmakers so hard that they were forced to scrap their plans to make it easier for corporations to fire younger workers.

There are other forces that catalyze change. Reporter and social commentator Malcolm Gladwell, in his best-selling book *The Tipping Point,* narrates the unexpected and circuitous routes sweeping change can take. He makes a convincing case that ideas and behavior can spread as quickly as infectious diseases—spreading from individual to individual, community to community, until they become widespread. Small factors can ultimately tip and have great consequences.

Individual voices across America's kitchen tables, not just the salons of New York and the policy institutes of Washington, can offer practical solutions. When Americans entered more than twenty-two thousand ideas in an SEIU-sponsored contest for the best ideas "Since Sliced Bread," our Web site (Since SlicedBread.com) received 50 million hits. For two months, on the Since Sliced Bread blog, citizens had extraordinarily civil conversations about how to solve the big problems facing America's working families. I am not sure that Filippo Menczer, a runner-up Since Sliced Bread winner from Bloomington, Indiana, would ever have dreamed that he would spark a conversation about minimum wage that would inspire Senator Hillary Clinton to introduce legislation to tie the minimum wage to congressional pay raises. That experience convinced me even more that a huge number of Americans are hungry for substantive conversations about the future and that they have their own good ideas about the changes our country needs to make.

There are other moments of change where the brave actions of an individual can be the spark that lights a bonfire of change.

- In 1977, Vaclav Havel, who later became the Czech president, organized a defense committee for a Czech rock band, called the Plastic People of the Universe, which morphed into the Charter 77 organization, which led to Czechoslovakia's broader democracy movement.
- Lech Walesa, a union activist scaling a wall to begin an occupation of the Gdansk Shipyard, defying the Kremlin, could not have fathomed that he was setting in motion the forces that would lead to Poland's independence and earn him a Nobel Prize.
- Mahatma Gandhi's civil disobedience against British authorities led to Indian independence.
- Nelson Mandela's resistance while incarcerated helped end apartheid.
- Ryan White, an unknown student until he was expelled from school after contracting AIDS, spent the six remaining years of his life educating others on the facts about HIV and AIDS and inspired Congress to name its funding for AIDS education the Ryan White Care Act.

None of these individuals was a well-known elected political leader. They had no schematics, computer programs, MapQuest directions, or crystal balls to guide them, but what they had was much more important. They had their conscience, their heart, soul, voice, and moral leadership. And no one could ever have predicted that they would reshape history.

No one would have predicted that one baseball player's arm casually draped over another player's shoulder could shape history. When Pee Wee Reese put his arm around Jackie Robinson, the African-American who integrated professional baseball, he made a symbolic gesture of support that sent a message of acceptance that spoke volumes to players and fans. Robinson, a change agent who endured indignities as a pathbreaker, said, "A life is not important, except in the impact it has on other lives."

In 1989, another symbolic act affected people across the globe: A brave man stood still and faced seventeen approaching tanks in Tiananmen Square, not knowing that his stance would become a worldwide symbol for the heroic fight for democracy in China. The photograph of that lone man, taken by Jeff Widener of the Associated Press, brought the students' struggle to the world, and led to intense moral outrage demanding an end to Chinese repression.

Of course, the possibility of effecting change is increased by the heightened attention received by odd couples—the pairing of Senator John McCain and Senator Ted Kennedy on immigration, former Speaker of the House Newt Gingrich and Senator Hillary Clinton on electronic medical records. Change can also be the product of out-of-character behavior: President Nixon going to China; Mitt Romney promoting universal health care; Ariel Sharon unilaterally pulling out of settlements in Gaza.

This is not to say that throwing out the current crowd running Washington is not important in making change. It is vitally important. Political leadership matters. The current leadership in the White House and Congress has pursued a foolhardy program to reward wealth, not work. But changing leaders alone, as I learned with the AFL-CIO, does not necessarily translate into new policies. All too often, political leadership follows rather than leads, so I never underestimate the power of people.

COMMON SENSE IDEAS

In 1776, Thomas Paine wrote in his treatise *Common Sense:*

> Perhaps the sentiments contained in the following pages, are not
> yet sufficiently fashionable to procure them general favour; a

long habit of not thinking a thing wrong, gives it a superficial appearance of being right, and raises at first a formidable outcry in defence of custom. But the tumult soon subsides. Time makes more converts than reason.

What is the common sense plan for America to reward work in the new economy? I don't mean a report from a congressional committee or an obscure federal agency. We need a vigorous and open discussion among Americans about the vision and the framework for our lives in the years ahead. Imagine a serious conversation about our nation's future without partisan rancor and impugning of motives—an honest, long-overdue American dialogue about the future of our country and the prospects for our children.

This requires us to open our minds to the unconventional or even the radical, and to welcome opinions, as Tom Paine put it, that are "not yet sufficiently fashionable to procure them general favour."

Many of the answers America needs are right in front of our eyes but they are hard to see when our leaders in Washington are engulfed in a fog. Today's negativity too often trumps future necessity. Listening to the Sunday-morning talk shows and insider political debates, one becomes anesthetized by talking heads analyzing congressional vote counts, budget reconciliation, deficits, party politics, and past failed legislation. They never seem to meet a new idea they like. "We can't do that, it's too complicated," they say, or, "Here's the problem with . . ." Such oft-repeated sentiments serve only to rationalize political paralysis.

I understand that every government program has a sponsor, every idea a nuance, every interest a lobbyist, and every policy a cost. I understand that the odds are stacked against change, as did Tom Paine more than two hundred years ago when he wrote that new directions " . . . raise at first a formidable outcry in defence of custom." Messengers of change who arouse the ire of one constituency or another are regularly thrashed for their hubris. "Idea assassins" emerge, as futurists Alvin and Heidi Toffler noted, to murder change by a thousand details or questions.

What follows here are my opinions about a plan for change. Most of the ideas are not really new and, in fact, many are not mine at all. But they all share two characteristics: First, they can work, and some are working already; second, they are not pipe dreams, but are both practical and principled. According to Newt Gingrich, success comes when we "Plan back from victory rather than forward from the present," and that is my intention.

I invite feedback and heated debate with all comers—workers, students, business executives, union members and leaders, association directors, and politicians. Let the debate begin in earnest because the challenges confronting us are pressing. Go to ACountryThatWorks.com and tell me what you think.

1. America Should Stop Taxing Hard Work and Start Rewarding It

A just nation should base its system of taxation on rewarding hard work, promoting fairness, and ensuring economic opportunity for all Americans. Unfortunately, the Social Security payroll tax, FICA, fails these tests—but a few simple fixes could convert it to help most hardworking Americans.

The Federal Insurance Contributions Act (FICA) is a regressive 7.65 percent payroll tax on Americans' hard work. Workers pay 6.2 percent into Social Security and an additional 1.45 percent into Medicare, with employers contributing an equal amount. For Social Security, there's a cap on wages subject to the tax, which was $94,200 in 2006 and rises slightly each year indexed to inflation. (For Medicare, there's no cap on wages subject to the tax.) Social Security was established as a form of insurance with a maximum benefit, and Congress set a cap on wages to keep some relationship between contributions and the benefits paid.

Payroll taxes have played an important role by providing the revenue to meet our nation's commitment to retirees, but it is time to rethink how we fund those obligations more equitably. I have already discussed how we are witnessing fast-growing income inequality, as top earners capture an ever greater share of the total wages earned by Americans. But because only the first $94,200 of wages is taxed, a growing percentage of income earned is not subject to the tax for Social Security. In 1983, Congress set that cap to target 90 percent of income earned, yet today the portion of the income pie subject to tax for Social Security has fallen to 84 percent.

There's a big problem with this: The Social Security tax is regressive, meaning that higher-paid workers earning over $94,200 stop paying FICA tax on any income in excess of the cap, while lower-wage workers—most Americans—must pay the tax on every single dollar they earn. In other words, someone earning $1 million a year pays the same amount in Social Security taxes as someone making $94,200.

We should create a Social Security system with a more broad-based funding mechanism that has individuals contributing more in line with their ability, starting with eliminating the cap on wages taxed. The Heritage Foundation estimates that simply eliminating the cap would raise approximately $607 billion in the first five years.

We should also correct a fundamental discrepancy within the FICA system. The FICA tax applies to income from wages; it does not apply to income from interest, dividends, or capital gains. Wealthy Americans get much of their income from those sources rather than wages—so they avoid paying FICA on that income while virtually all of average workers' income is in wages that do require FICA payments. This contributes tremendously to the regressive nature of the FICA tax, and does not support the principle of rewarding work. Let's end the wage-tax-only operating assumption of FICA, and treat all income equally by applying the FICA tax to income from dividends, capital gains, stock options, and interest. Individuals with higher incomes from multiple sources will then pay FICA on all income.

And here's another idea to make this system better reward work: Let's take the income raised by removing the cap on Social Security (approximately $1.4 trillion in ten years) and add the additional revenue we would raise by treating all income (wages, dividends, capital gains, etc,) equally, and use these savings, and other revenue sources, if necessary, to exempt the first $50,000 in income from FICA tax (or, if we're feeling gutsy, the first $100,000). Meanwhile, we should continue the annual cost-of-living indexing to raise the cap in line with inflation. FICA payroll taxes would thus kick in on all income earned *over* $50,000, a far more equitable way to make work pay.

2. An American Health Care Plan

The employer-based health care system is dying. Despite spending 16 percent of our Gross Domestic Product (GDP) on health care, the system is hopelessly broken. The percentage of our GDP being spent on health care is rising: Every day fewer Americans have health care coverage or pay more for it because employers are annually increasing copays, deductibles, and premiums. There are not just cost problems but quality issues as well. The Institute of Medicine reports that 98,000 hospitalized Americans die every year, and 1 million more are injured as a result of preventable medical errors. Hospital administrators I talk with say there is far too great an occurrence of people getting sicker while in hospitals.

Employer-based health care is a relic of the domestic industrial economy, and employers today are competing in a global economy. It is in the economic self-interest of American business, now competing globally, to end employer-based care. Employer-based health care served America well for a long time, and may it rest in peace. Precious time is being lost trying to patch it up by making incremental fixes focusing on one subpopulation or one type of benefit or one disease. Our imperative is to rapidly find a twenty-first-century American model so we can create a much more effective system. Opposition to changing our system is fierce, but the more compelling and clear the alternative, the greater the public support will be to mobilize behind it.

Corporate leaders, who have failed to embrace health care reform, need now to shout out for change. American culture makes it unlikely that our country will import wholesale some other country's health care system. But that's not a problem because surrounding us right here in the United States we can find all the ingredients for a new plan.

Step 1 is to create a system that has as its foundation the same basic tenet as our educational system: universal access. *If every child is guaranteed a public education, every American must be guaranteed access to affordable health care.* Then we can integrate the finest research, doctors, and hospitals in the world into a delivery system that controls costs and offers the highest quality.

Step 2 is to build a consensus that a new health care plan must do the following:

- Cover all Americans.
- Ensure a choice of doctors and health care plans.
- Include preventative care as part of any basic benefit.
- Control costs.
- Utilize electronic medical records that patients control.
- Require hospital and physician quality, outcome, and cost data to be made available to patients.
- Integrate long-term care services and costs into the system to maximize people's opportunities to stay at home.
- Allow for employers, individuals, and government to share in the financing of the system.

Step 3 is the best news: There are plenty of models to adopt or adapt.

There's nothing wrong with the most obvious of these: the health plan our president, 535 members of Congress, and approximately 9 million federal employees rely on. The Federal Employee Benefit Health Plan (FEBHP) offers a basic benefit, a choice of plans and options (fee for service, point of service, and HMOs), and allocates an amount of money, based on a formula, to each federal worker. If a plan's participant wants more coverage, lower copays, or special benefits, they can spend more of their own money. The American College of Physicians, American Society of Internal Medicine and the Democratic Leadership Council's Progressive Policy Institute have called for an expansion of the Federal Employee Benefits Program to allow Americans the opportunity to participate.

If the FEBHP system leaves you cold for some reason, try the military's TRICARE system. TRICARE is the Department of Defense's health care program for more than 9 million members of the uniformed services and their families and survivors, and retired members and their families. TRICARE processes 8.5 million health care claims per month on average, electronic claims are paid in five days, and over 98 percent of claims are processed within thirty days. TRICARE integrates civilian hospitals into their plans and had no premium increases from 2000–2004. TRICARE could also be a platform to scale up to a larger population.

Why not extend it to others?

Want it even simpler? Extend Medicare coverage to every man, woman, and child. Why not Medicare for All? Medicare is far more efficient than private health care. It has administrative costs under 3 percent, compared to private insurance plans that, on average, spend about 9.5 percent of total costs for administration.

Still unsure? Take a road trip to Vermont and Massachusetts, two states with new, nearly universal plans, or talk with former governor of Oregon and health care innovator Dr. John Kitzhaber, who believes he can provide nearly universal coverage for Oregonians if the state could get waivers from the federal government to more flexibly use federal funds in conjunction with state, employer, and individual resources.

The government could design a national health care initiative by providing broad parameters (setting a basic preventative-benefit package, national catastrophic coverage, information on best practices, transparency on costs, opportunities for group purchasing, standards for privacy, and portability of electronic records), and then empowering states to tailor unique plans to fit the needs of their citizens—with the federal government sharing in the financing.

If you doubt that such a system would work, consider that all of the following countries currently have some style of universal health care: Australia, Austria, Belgium, Canada, Cuba, Denmark, Finland, France, Germany, Japan, The Netherlands, New Zealand, Norway, Taiwan, and the United Kingdom, and they spend at least 5 percent less of their GDPs on health care. Some countries have restrictions that I don't like, such as too long a wait for nonemergency procedures or inadequate dental services, but many have lower health care costs and better health outcomes. Because the United States would be building something from scratch, we could import the best of each country's system.

If all of these nations can figure out universal plans that meet their nations' interests, why can't America do the same? Americans deserve *a fair debate, not an endless one* on how best to provide universal, affordable, quality health care. Our political leaders need a grand vision and a passion to get the job done, and they'll find a receptive country. According to a survey commissioned by the Center for American Progress and Americans for Health Care, nine out of ten Americans (89 percent) say " . . . with costs rising out of control and the quality of health coverage declining, the health care system in our country is broken, and we need to make fundamental changes."

"Of all the forms of inequality, injustice in health care is the most shocking and inhumane," declared Martin Luther King Jr.

3. America Needs a New Retirement System

The employer-employee relationship, like a marriage, has many mutual benefits, if each side lives up to its responsibilities. Unfortunately, when it comes to retirement, America's employers seem eager to divorce the workers who have labored long and hard for them. This spells big trouble for Americans' retirement security.

Workers and retirees at Enron, WorldCom, Global Crossing, Rite Aid, and other companies have seen their retirement security vanish along with the 401(k)s they had that were heavily weighted with company stock. We've seen airlines and steel companies go into bankruptcy court and, virtually overnight, gut the pension promises that their employees had relied on.

As pointed out earlier, fewer workers in the private sector are covered by defined-benefit pension plans under which employers provide workers with a guaranteed level of retirement income (normally based on years of service and pay level). Only about 34 million workers today are covered by defined-benefit pensions—just under a quarter of the U.S. workforce.

- Today, *more than half* of all workers do not have *any* retirement benefit other than Social Security.
- According to a recent study conducted by Fidelity Investments, the median American family is on track to replace only 57 percent of their income after they retire, meaning that retirees will need to figure out how to live on 40 percent less income after retirement.

These retirement-savings and pension-coverage numbers are woefully low—retirees do not have the security of knowing they will not outlive their assets, which heaps additional anxiety on families already struggling to make ends meet. Current and soon-to-be retirees are contending with the possibility of needing to work until they die, praying that their health will even allow them to do so. This cannot be—we must create new retirement arrangements that maximize the chance for each American to retire in dignity with financial security.

In the past, for most working Americans, a secure retirement relied on three pillars: paying off their mortgage by retirement; a pension from their employer; and Social Security. Once upon a time, some workers also had money saved.

But home equity loans have converted homes into piggy banks to be borrowed against for current living expenses. Defined-benefit-guaranteed employer pensions, as I noted, are becoming a relic of the past. And thank God—*or Franklin D. Roosevelt*—for Social Security, which while it could be improved, still is the only guaranteed benefit workers can trust.

The first task in constructing a new system is to establish a minimum goal, that is a percentage of current income on which Americans could securely retire. Financial planners generally recommend that retirement income be enough to replace 70–85 percent of one's income at the time of retirement through pensions, Social Security, investments, and savings. Individuals need to be aware from their first employment of the advantages of long-term saving and the amount of money they will need to set aside to meet a reasonable rate of replacement of their pre-retirement income. Policy makers need to help people understand financial planning, encourage long-term asset accumulation, facilitate savings, and assist in ensuring the funding of retirement.

The second task is to establish the principles of a solid retirement plan:

- **Lifetime contributions.** Contributions should be made over the course of an individual's entire work life. Financially healthy employers should be required to contribute a basic, predictable, and stable amount to their employees' retirement coverage. The advantages of regular savings can be seen in the following investment savings examples:

Assuming an 8% annual return:

- At birth, a child is given $1,000, which is invested in an account earning 8% for 70 years: $218,606.41.
- At birth, a child contributes $50 a month into an account earning 8% for 70 years: $1,987,905.09.
- An individual starts investing at age 25, and contributes $50 a month into an account earning 8% until age 70: $263,726.99.
- A 25-year-old makes a onetime contribution of $1,000 to an investment account earning 8% until he is 70 years old: $31,920.45.

- **Guaranteed and predictable employer contributions.** Employers should be required to contribute to their employees' retirement coverage and the contribution rate must be predictable and stable. If we do not want government and individuals to be the only contributors to retirement security, we must have employers, at least large ones, pay a minimum defined contribution to an employee account, and respect employees' existing earned defined-benefit obligations.
- **No withdrawals during one's work life.** No cash-out provisions should be allowed while working, other than for rare emergencies. There should be a cap on withdrawals and repayment-requirement policies.
- **Guaranteed lifetime benefits and limited cash out.** Lump-sum cash payouts would be limited (maybe to 20 percent) at the time of retirement. The remainder of the account would remain as a secure lifetime annuity paying a monthly guaranteed payment.
- **Matching employee contributions.** Supplemental employees' contributions should be matched by their employer on a predetermined ratio of perhaps dollar-to-dollar, with a cap.

And maybe we should have an obligatory employee contribution of some percentage of pay for workers making above the poverty rate, particularly if we change FICA as discussed.

- **Portable accounts.** An individual's retirement account should be portable across all employers during his or her work life. Once an individual account is created, the money is exclusively the asset of the employee, and he or she should be able to obtain the value of this retirement account on a regular basis.

- **Pooled investment risk.** Any system should minimize administrative costs and pool and professionally manage assets in order to control investment risk across a large number of participants and employers. Unions, associations, financial institutions, and other certified organizations should be lifetime intermediaries that act as fiduciaries, offer a minimum range of approved investment options, have financial-planning capabilities for participants, set maximum fees that can be charged, and allow individuals complete control and transparency on fees, their investments, and their accounts.

Is this type of new American retirement system a pipe dream? Not for the fifteen-thousand-plus nonprofit and educational institutions that use TIAA-CREF, one of the largest financial services companies in the United states. TIAA-CREF, with $360 billion in assets, is by far the largest manager of so-called employer-sponsored 403(b) tax-sheltered annuity plans. It offers 401(k), 457, and Keogh plans, mutual funds, after-tax annuities, and life insurance, 529 college savings plans, Coverdell Education Savings Accounts, financial planning, and trust and investment management. TIAA-CREF participants are able to have different employers pay into one account, switch jobs and take their pensions with them, and receive—through a low-cost annuity—a guaranteed defined benefit at retirement. And it allows for employer contributions—a critical component for building the assets necessary for a secure retirement.

Even President Bush's controversial proposal for Social Security personal accounts—which was fatally flawed because it proposed to fund the accounts by transferring money out of Social Security's pooled, insured, and guaranteed benefit into personal, uninsured, nonguaranteed benefit accounts—included a way for individuals to invest in one account throughout their work lives. Add employer contributions to the personal accounts, and the ability at retirement to purchase low-cost insured annuities (lifetime-guaranteed payments) and, voila, a new universal plan.

For a good example of improved retirement security in action today, we should cross the globe to Australia. While the United States is thinking about a twenty-first-century model for retirement, Australia has created one. It's called Superannuation. The program requires employers to make contributions of 9 percent of an employee's base pay into that employee's Superannuation fund every three months, which is invested until retirement. Many funds also grant some coverage if an employee becomes unable to work due to illness or accident, and pay benefits to beneficiaries upon the employee's death.

In addition to this stability, the Superannuation program allows for quite a bit of individual flexibility: Individual workers can make contributions to their own funds, transfer them from employer to employer, and choose from a variety of investment programs to suit their individual tolerance for risk and need for customer service. But, most important, employers are required to pay into their employees' accounts every three months, guaranteeing a steady stream of contributions over the working life of each employee.

The critical point is that American workers should not have to cobble together a solution that looks like Australia's by rolling over 401(k)s and only choosing to work for employers that make matching contributions. Australia's system is portable, compulsory, and capable of providing the pillar of retirement security that workers desperately need; it is not a defined-benefit plan like Social Security, but by purchasing annuities at retirement it can act like one. However, given that only 48 percent of Americans participate in *any* kind of employer-based retirement plan, a program like Superannuation would go a long way toward providing retirement stability to American workers.

Here's another idea from across an ocean: We could import a version of England's Child Trust Fund, in which all children born since 2002 receive £250 (about $470 US) from the government in their personal savings account at birth, with the children of low-income families receiving £500 (about $940 US). At age seven, the government pays in an additional £250, and again, those with lower incomes receive £500. Parents can contribute more if they are able and willing, up to £1,200 per year. There is no tax on investment gains in the account. Parents can choose from among plans that have stock exposure and those that operate like savings accounts. The money can be used for anything—education, a down payment on a home—whatever is needed when the child turns eighteen.

After Social Security and private savings, the third key to a secure retirement is home equity. For all the talk about savings, most working Americans' homes, if they are lucky enough to own one, are their biggest asset. The faster homeowners pay off their mortgage's principal, the more equity they build. Why not provide the same tax breaks for paying down a home mortgage principal under the same conditions and limitations as IRAs or 401(k)s? Under this proposal, the money invested in a home can come from pretax income, and the money cannot be withdrawn without tax penalties in the form of a home equity loan or other cash-out until the owner has reached a certain age. If principal payments were protected, and withdrawals limited, we might accelerate home ownership, as people would save more in order to own more of the homes they live in rather than other investments.

Owning more equity in your home opens up another opportunity for retirement income: reverse mortgages. This option is rapidly growing in popularity—whereas only 150 reverse mortgages took place in 1990, in 2005 forty-three thousand homeowners took advantage of the equity they built in their homes to supplement their incomes.

A reverse mortgage is a loan against the equity in a home that enables the owner to receive payments each month for as long as he or she lives there. Reverse mortgages have a different purpose than a traditional mortgage: With a forward or traditional mortgage, income is used to repay debt, and this builds up equity.

With a reverse mortgage, the lender sends the owner cash, and he or she makes no repayments. As debt grows, equity will shrink (unless your home's value is growing at a high rate). That is exactly why informed reverse-mortgage borrowers want to "spend down" their home equity while they live in their homes, without having to make monthly loan repayments.

If you are sixty-five today and have a home worth $200,000, you could receive $582 per month for as long as you live in your home, or, for $500,000 worth of equity, you could receive over your lifetime approximately $1,090 a month.

Payments begin after retirement or a preset age, and homeowners receive payments for life. If they pass away before the loan is paid off, the remainder of the equity passes to their heirs, but if they outlive their equity, the bank still makes the monthly payments.

As Americans' life expectancy increases, building equity in one's home more quickly creates security and a wide array of options. We should make it easier to pay off the mortgage through tax-sheltered payment opportunities, so that homeowners can build their equity more rapidly and take advantage of the financial strength that owning a home can offer.

4. From the Interstate to the Internet Highway

The Interstate Highway System, birthed in the 1950s, now includes over 42,700 miles of roads from coast to coast and border to border. The highway system was promoted by President Eisenhower to meet new peacetime national-security needs, troop and civilian movement in case of attack, and growing commerce. In the vibrant postwar industrial economy, the highway system expanded the economic transport of goods from private railways to public roadways.

But in a global economy, the basis of commerce is no longer just the transfer of goods; it's the transfer of information. The Internet is today's global infrastructure and it is vital to America's global competitiveness, which requires instantaneous information sharing among government, business, and service providers such as lawyers, accountants, and suppliers—not to mention our personal communication with our doctors, teachers, and family. Access to the Internet is a prerequisite for equal opportunity for kids, and pricing parents off-line is bad public policy.

Investing in the Internet highway is far easier, quicker, and inexpensive than building our interstate road system. San Francisco Mayor Gavin Newsom is readying to make his city a wireless town that would allow any person with a recent computer and a wireless modem to access the Internet for free. As Newsom said when he announced his program: "It is to me a fundamental right to have access universally to information . . . This is a civil rights issue as much as anything else."

All American citizens—rich and poor—need equal access to the electronic highway to travel the roads of the twenty-first century, but so does American business if we are going to have the infrastructure to compete in a global economy.

5. A World-Class Education System and a School of One
Americans have spent more time studying, discussing, measuring, and hand-wringing about their children's education than anyone can quantify. It's hard to keep up with the flurry of education trends and ideas, but the bottom line is clear: We are still leaving too many children behind, particularly in our urban

schools. According to the Urban Institute, "Students from historically disadvantaged minority groups (American Indian, Hispanic, Black) have little more than a fifty-fifty chance of finishing high school with a diploma." For all the fanfare of the No Child Left Behind Act (NCLB), the reality falls far short of the hype. According to the American Federation of Teachers, "Congress knew that the goals of NCLB could not be achieved without accountability and additional resources and it set a funding authorization for NCLB for each year. For Title I, the cornerstone of NCLB, the authorization for 2006 is $22.75 billion. But President Bush has only requested $13.3 billion of that total for this vital program."

Pre-K to 12—America's Future

I am not an expert on education policy, but I do have some ideas for teaching our young children.

An adequate education system for the twenty-first century must include universal pre-kindergarten, beginning at the age of four. Or better yet, why not at age two? The Committee for Economic Development estimates that universal pre-kindergarten education for all three- and four-year-olds would require $25 to $35 billion if implemented all at one time. Georgia and Oklahoma and a few other states have already implemented universal pre-K. Countless studies document that brain development and critical learning occur at very early stages of childhood. According to the National Head Start Association, every dollar invested in early intervention pays off. A study of over six hundred Head Start graduates from San Bernardino County, California, reports that for every dollar spent, society receives over eight dollars in benefits.

Education from pre-kindergarten through twelfth grade needs to be enshrined as this century's basic education entitlement; early childhood education is not a luxury but a national responsibility. And with more two-income working families today, a safe, free, publicly financed place for their child to learn and play while their parents work is a growing necessity for parents' emotional and economic peace of mind.

Small Schools

School systems, like other mass organizations of the twentieth century, face the challenge of reinventing themselves, and smaller schools are critical to the twenty-first century. Middle schools and high schools with too many students aren't conducive to learning. In 2005, Bill Gates, chairman of Microsoft, reported to our nations' governors that "students in smaller schools are more motivated, have higher attendance rates, feel safer, and graduate and attend college in higher numbers." The Chicago Public School System reports that its research on small schools shows:

> There is almost 40 years of existing research and literature on small schools which indicates that students in small schools have higher attendance and graduation rates, fewer drop-outs, equal or better levels of academic achievement (standardized test scores, course failure rates, grade point averages), higher levels of extra-curricular participation and parent involvement, and fewer incidences of discipline and violence.

Studies also show that smaller schools have higher graduation rates and lower dropout rates than larger schools. Large schools should be broken up into smaller units or smaller schools. When it comes to schools, big is not better.

A School of One

The computer and the Internet are the most exciting educational assets available, and the most underutilized educational tools in America.

When my son was younger, I couldn't keep him off the computer. Math games, skills tests, reading about ocean creatures, and, of course, video games occupied him for hours on end. Then he went to school. Computers were down the hall in "labs," not in classrooms. Teachers lectured and handed out photocopied worksheets. Like many kids, Matt was lost and having trouble in his traditional classroom, yet he was intellectually stimulated at home.

The Internet is the classroom "textbook" in the knowledge economy and provides the paradigm-busting opportunity for kids to learn at their own speed, tailored to their own needs. A "School of One" is now at hand. Why aren't teachers using the tools that could transform education from a mass production to a personalized education system? Almost all public schools have Internet access, yet few take advantage of it. One reason is that in most schools, computers tend to be isolated in computer rooms down the hall from most classrooms, rather than centrally connected to regular classroom activities.

Teachers should be guides to this vast storehouse of knowledge, direct students to great online lectures, structure time for individual student challenges, and develop for each student School of One learning plans. Computers can facilitate the giving and grading of tests, providing homework assignments and reading lists, maintaining and transmitting attendance lists, ordering supplies, and sending notes to parents.

Experts at McKinsey & Company, advisers to some of America's most successful companies, prepared for the National Information Infrastructure Advisory Council (NIIAC)—a council of citizens and stakeholders created by executive order of President Clinton to focus on public-and private-technology issues—a report on how technology and education could be integrated. Imagine:

> . . . this typical morning at your kids middle school connected to the information superhighway. One group of students arrives early to update the school's home page on the World Wide Web. Meantime, the principal is reviewing the electronic mail that parents sent her the evening before, prior to sending voice

mail to all her teachers suggesting a schedule for the upcoming parent-teacher "open house." Later in the morning, in a first-period modern history class, the same video technology that carried the local morning broadcast now enables this class to tour the Smithsonian's aerospace [Air and Space] museum. In the classroom next door, the subject is anthropology. Students are grouped in teams of 3 and 4 around the classroom's computers, engrossed in a computer simulation that allows them to play the role of archaeologists on-site in Egypt, exploring ancient Egyptian culture as revealed in its artifacts. In the classroom down the hall, each individual student is working math problems *pitched at exactly the pace and level of difficulty appropriate for him or her,* and getting immediate feedback on the answers, thanks to interactive software . . . (emphasis added)

It sounds like an interesting day for the students, not to mention the flexibility and convenience it offers teachers of being able to - online and 24/7 - administer standardized testing, grade multiple-choice assignments, or access world-class curricula. And computers have another outstanding characteristic—they are perpetually patient and available.

It seems plausible, more enjoyable, and, according to McKinsey & Company, Inc, eminently possible. Through open-sourcing to reduce software costs, and the purchase of basic computers in bulk—for as little as $150 each—America's 50 million students could have their own computers every five years at a total cost of roughly $1.5 billion annually. It seems quite feasible when the cost is compared to the $440 billion annually spent overall on K–12 education budget, and you could probably pay for the initiative simply from the reduction in the cost of textbooks as virtual information online replaces hard copy. And a bonus: Kids with computers at home have higher grade-point averages, and that trend would hopefully continue as poorer students gain access.

The same study done by McKinsey & Company showed

that the cost of connecting every classroom in every public K–12 school by 2005, including professional development for teachers, would have represented only 3.9 percent of the projected 2005 education budget in the first year, but after the front-end investment, its proportion in the budget would drop to around 1.5 percent to pay for Internet connections, upkeep, upgrades, and new programs.

An additional investment of less than 4 percent would add telephones with voice mail features and business-quality video capability to the classroom, facilitating communication with guest lecturers, other teachers or educational experts. It could also allow teachers and administrators to receive from and leave messages for parents and students.

It seems like a reasonable price to build a platform that would permit either cost reductions or the reallocation of resources as large numbers of headquarter-based personnel are reduced. Computers and Internet capability could facilitate or eliminate the following functions: headquarter-staff-developed curriculum; testing; attendance-record keeping; purchasing, the distribution of policies and information; and the updating of personnel records.

6. Skills Training and Post–Secondary Education Training

Be All That You Can Be

"Be All That You Can Be," one of the U.S. Army's recruiting slogans, represents the best ideal of America. Having the opportunity to achieve one's highest potential is what we all seek for ourselves and our children.

But how can America ensure that college education and skill development are available prior to your work life? Ask yourself: Are there models of integrated education and skills training? What about the army, where you trade service to your country for an education? Why shouldn't young people have the doors of opportunity opened if they want to serve their country for extended periods of time? Why can't they receive training during their service and an education award upon completion?

When Hurricane Katrina struck land, I think it would have been beneficial if we had not had to rely completely on an overextended military, including the National Guard or FEMA for the front line of disaster relief. Why doesn't America have an emergency disaster corps of young people enlisted to serve their country in emergencies such as hurricanes, floods, forest fires, and other natural disasters? How about trading service for education for people who want to be tutors and mentors in failing urban schools? Or, help seniors live independently in their homes, act as aides in nursing homes, or assist in homeland security duties? Why not implement a national program available to all interested students with the same educational opportunities as volunteers for national service in the army? We could provide a wide range of educational opportunities during service, and an AmeriCorps-type award of ten thousand dollars a year upon completion, which could go a long way to help lower-income families pay college tuition.

In the army, each recruit makes his or her own education plan, choosing from an array of options from basic skills to graduate level education:

- The army's Basic Skills Program gives soldiers job-related training to improve their ability to perform their jobs as effectively as possible.
- The army's High School Completion Program (HSCP) offers soldiers and their family members the chance to earn a high-school degree or certificate of equivalency.
- The army's Continuing Education Services (ACES) encourages lifelong learning, with tuition assistance, in order to help soldiers continue to update their skills.
- The Web site eArmyU.com describes an array of educational services, including tuition assistance.
- Service members Opportunity Colleges (SOC) is a coali-

tion of education associations whose goal is to address the higher-education needs of its members in the armed services.

Why can't all Americans who serve their country have their own education plans and the same type of choices the army has developed, and then have the resources to continue on afterward so that all Americans can be all that they can be?

"BUT . . ."

I can almost hear what some of you are thinking: But what about the . . . ? How could . . . ? Would it change . . . ? How much . . . ? Can it pass the . . . ? And of course, how much does it cost?

The answers begin with a question: Would America work better if we stop taxing work, reinvent our health care and retirement systems, connect everyone to the Internet highway, educate our children from pre-K through twelfth grade, use technology to create a School of One, and offer high school graduates the chance to exchange national service for education? And these are just a few of the many possibilities out there.

I unequivocally think the answer is yes. If you agree, then the real question is how to overcome the obstacles and get these things done. Will that be easy? Of course not. Is it possible? I believe it is. Especially with the right vision. There's a quotation from Helen Keller I love: "The most pathetic person in the world is someone who has sight, but has no vision." Vision is the starting point from which we plan backward. Seeing without vision results in an organization or nation running around with lots of activity but little progress.

It is impossible to reshape our country—any more than it is to reshape a union or business or political party—without disrupting the status quo. Change is not a zero-sum game. There are winners and losers. Simply building a health care system on top of the old one or adding new technological tools to our classrooms without revising how we educate our children would be programmatically unrealistic and financially disastrous.

America is going to have to make hard choices to end or consolidate what we now do and trade in the old for what we want to do. The focus of my first year as SEIU president was restructuring and eliminating many longstanding programs and services to aggregate the resources to fund SEIU's new vision. At SEIU we doubled dues, restructured locals, and ended services—all actions that previously were considered taboo. But our members shared a vision of a union that could change their lives and they were willing to make the tough choices to pay for it. As one leader said, "You can't have a champagne union with beer money." A similar overhaul is needed for our government.

Policy experts have probably been reading this with their calculators in hand, totaling costs and preparing to assassinate these ideas as fiscally irresponsible. Even a close friend of mine, after reading an early draft of my ideas, remarked, "I know you told me to think about the policy proposals—don't angst over the cost—but how much does it cost?" A lot of money, just like the war in Iraq, the new prescription drug plan, or rebuilding New Orleans. Big decisions cost big money.

I do not have detailed calculations of the costs of the programs I've proposed, but I invite policy makers to let me know what they think. Let's get the figures on the table and then the American public will be able to decide if these programs are worth the costs. Before we budget for new programs, we should consider ways to consolidate spending on current programs, or eliminate programs no longer necessary. We need to make choices as to how we will pay for the new programs.

The financial answers are not hard to find. They are also all around us.

RAISING REVENUE

To gain passage for the programs I've advocated, we've got to find ways to finance them. Funds can be generated by operating more efficiently—consolidation and elimination of today's government programs—but there's no question that special funding will be needed. Here are a few ways to raise the cash and estimated revenues:

Tax Corporations Appropriately

In the United States, the federal tax rate on corporate income for the largest corporations is set at 35 percent. This seems straightforward, so one would assume that the staggering growth in corporate profits over the past twenty years would result in ever-higher corporate contributions to federal revenues. However, a closer look at the amount of taxes that corporations actually pay reveals a staggeringly different picture. In 2005, the share of the Gross Domestic Income in 2005 comprising corporate profits (as compared to workers' wages) was at its highest level in thirty-seven years. Yet, corporate tax revenues as a share of the federal budget have shrunk tremendously: From 28 percent in the 1950s and 21 percent in the 1960s, to 10 percent in the 1980s and have *collapsed to a mere 2 percent today!* What's more, a recent study that examined the financial standing of 275 of the companies listed on the 2004 Fortune 500 list found that while pretax corporate profits for those 275 companies rose by 26 percent from 2001 to 2003, the amount those corporations paid in taxes actually *fell* by 21 percent over those same years. Something is seriously out of whack.

How would we begin to close the gap between what corporations earn and how much they pay in taxes? To begin, let's tackle the ways that American corporations shield money from the

IRS by sheltering it abroad. For example, U.S. companies frequently use accounting techniques to allocate income to countries with lower tax rates. We could raise approximately $8 billion in revenue per year simply by deciding that U.S. companies that earn money abroad have to pay taxes on those profits.

Similarly, if we decided to close the loopholes that allow U.S. corporations to shift their earnings to foreign tax shelters (the so-called Bermuda Loophole), we could realize another $2.6 billion in yearly tax revenues. Even without those simple proposals, just *defining* what a tax shelter is, so that the IRS and the Treasury Department can apply a single standard to the cases they examine, would raise $13 billion, to say nothing of the savings in reduced enforcement costs if the IRS didn't have to decide on a case-by-case basis whether companies hiding their earnings abroad constituted "tax sheltering."

Once that's done, let's close the loopholes and special tax breaks that profitable large corporations enjoy here at home and make them pay their share of taxes. Here's a mind-blowing statistic: There were eighty-two profitable companies that made $101 billion from 2001 to 2004, and yet in one or more of those years each of those companies paid absolutely nothing in taxes. Had they paid just the 35 percent corporate rate, the government would have earned another $35+ billion. In fact, many of them received substantial tax *breaks* from the government in those years—so many breaks that their total tax rebate from the IRS in the years they paid nothing in taxes came to *$12 billion.* Without our most successful companies paying their fair share of our nation's costs, individual taxpayers and the U.S. Treasury are left to foot the bill.

Corporate welfare is another way that the federal budget runs seriously off track. Every year, U.S. taxpayers spend billions and billions of dollars helping the Wal-Marts and General Electrics and Exxon-Mobils of the world expand markets overseas, relocate businesses within the United States, build roads to enhance their corporate headquarters, subsidize research and development programs—you name the subsidy, and you can find a member of Congress willing to slip it into a spending bill. Ending corporate welfare is an issue that can generate bipartisan appeal: Senator John McCain has proposed establishing a corporate welfare commission that would investigate the one hundred or more programs that he says transfer $65 billion from the federal budget to corporations every year. In his words, "terminating even some of these programs could save taxpayers tens of billions of dollars a year." Even the low estimates—a savings of $30 billion—are quite substantial.

And for good measure, since corporations pay handsomely to secure all these loopholes and special provisions, why not at least tax them for their trouble? I propose that we enact a use or sales tax on lawyers, accountants, consultants, and other business services. (I can hear the K Street lobbyists rumbling from here.) A few states have been tossing this idea around. Washington State's Department of Revenue calculates that extending the retail sales tax to professional, business, and financial services would raise revenues by $2 billion. And if applying the retail sales tax to all services uniformly doesn't work, then extending it to just five categories of business and professional services that corporations use (advertising, computer/data processing, miscellaneous business services/consulting, legal, engineering/architectural) would yield an additional $714 million in Washington State alone, so nationally the income would be substantial.

Tax Individual Incomes
and Wealth Appropriately

Having focused our attention on how corporations can pay taxes on par with their profits, we should now turn our attention to the challenges on the individual income side. We could make our tax system both more just and more robust if we pursued this set of initiatives:

- First and foremost, let's roll back the Bush tax cuts for those who make over $200,000 a year. With those cuts, the very epitome of the failed doctrine of trickle-down economics, we would have added about $290 billion to the federal deficit alone in 2004. Raising just the top two tax brackets by 1 percent would raise over $32.7 billion in five years. Simply restoring the top marginal income tax rate to 39.6 percent would raise $129.4 billion from 2006 to 2010.
- Second, we need to bring the tax rates on dividends and capital gains up to the ordinary rates for income taxes. Wealthy individuals draw much of their income from dividends and capital gains rather than actual income; therefore, maintaining these taxes at lower levels than income taxes is the mark of a highly regressive system. Just by restoring the dividends and capital gains taxes to their pre-2003 levels, we could raise $125 billion from 2006 to 2010.
- Third, it turns out that the difference between what taxpayers should be paying in taxes and how much they actually are evading is quite large: $345 billion per year. This is revenue that we need, and we should ensure that the IRS has the tools required to raise compliance and close the tax gap.
- Finally in a perfect world, we would replace the estate tax with an inheritance tax that, as the Tax Policy Center suggests, " ... would treat inheritances and gifts above some lifetime exemption as heirs' taxable income subject to progressive income tax rates." Instead of repealing the estate tax, as currently planned in 2010, we could exempt $2 million from an individual's estate, set the tax rate at 45 percent, and add $26 billion a year to the U.S. Treasury in 2011 alone.

Anteing Up for Big Ideas

As a nation, we face massive shared challenges. It is incumbent on all of us to do our part to tackle these problems, such as fixing our failing schools, bringing down the rising numbers of uninsured, and connecting everyone to the Internet highway. In addition to the revenues that we could raise by more progressively and appropriately taxing corporations and individuals, we as a society can choose to commit our resources to solving these problems more directly.

If we implemented a Value Added Tax (or some other form of consumption tax) and dedicated the revenue raised to solving just one of these problems, we could forever change the landscape of U.S. social policy. Budget analysts from the Congressional Research Service estimate that a broad-based Value Added Tax would have raised $37.9 billion in 2000 for each 1 percent tax levied. If we implemented a Value Added Tax of 3 to 4 percent with targeted exemptions (e.g., for small businesses, food purchases, education, dues to religious organizations, and health care services), we could raise between $100 billion and $160 billion a year. Dedicating that money to covering the uninsured, or using it as a core revenue in a national health insurance program, would go a long way to repairing the giant inequities in health care that we have sustained for too long.

Recent events should prove to us that we need to wean ourselves off our addiction to oil. We could decide as a society to take proactive steps in this direction by raising taxes on energy use, oil extraction, and CO_2 emissions (with rebates for low-income families and those in rural areas) and channeling that money directly to investments in our renewable energy infrastructure.

We don't lack big ideas that raise revenue and tackle our biggest social challenges simultaneously. Journalist and Senior Fellow at the Center for American Progress, Matt Miller has suggested what he calls "The 2% Solution," where just two cents on the national dollar would allow us to provide health insurance for all, guarantee full-time employees a living wage, and retool our educational system—all with a government a size that conservatives could love. All this for $220 billion per year—it sounds like quite the deal.

*   *   *

Americans must choose between what is good for the country as a whole and the interests of any individual or constituency.

While growing up, my mom wisely counseled: to get what you need means not getting everything you want. I bet on Americans' common sense. Every day at dinner tables, and late at night while sitting alone staring at the bills, working Americans make tough financial choices. Achieving a new health care plan or more computers in smaller schools will require an examination of other costly government initiatives and a decision regarding which is more important. Our citizens are wise enough to know that life is full of hard choices and they are ready to make them.

Conclusion

This fall my son, Matt, left home for the first time to go to college. He left me behind and now our two-bedroom nest is half empty. Change is inevitable.

I am so proud of Matt. Before he went to college he showed his growing personal responsibility by working full time at a bookstore by day and took classes at a local community college by night. As Cassie gave my life courage, Matt gives it purpose.

All parents have dreams for their kids and realistic goals for themselves. Parents are ready and willing to make important sacrifices for their children's dreams and for the American Dream. A country that works would adopt as its core mission the goal of making those dreams come true.

Americans understand that hard work and personal responsibility are the foundation of our economy. People want a hand up, not a hand out—a chance to rise as high as their abilities can take them. Families want to live comfortably. They want to be able to pay their bills and put food on the table—without the recurring monthly worry that they won't have enough to cover their expenses. Or that an unexpected health crisis would empty their bank accounts.

Americans expect their government to work for them, opening the doors of success and ensuring basic fairness for everyone. American workers grasp that the world and work are changing from 9-to-5 to 24/7, and that global competition is forcing employers to change as well. Workers hope their employers will treat them as assets, not as unnecessary costs in the balance sheet of change.

What Americans wish for is not that complicated, and, luckily, the answers surround us. What is missing is the passion and national political will—the great winds of change—to shape a new American plan for our economy, a way for America to ride the unending waves of change safely to shore.

Americans should pause and take the time to appreciate the glory and grandness of our future. *Humanity faces a quantum leap forward, and we are engaged in building a remarkable new civilization for the ground up.* No single generation has ever been offered such possibilities; we should seize them with passion and zest.

That is the panorama for America's future. Yet, how far into the distance can our country see? To the next election or further, to the next generations? If the first six years of this new century are any measure, America is forsaking hardworking Americans.

Leaders of all parties, occupations, associations, and institutions have so far failed to come together to harness the energy of our times. Yes, change is inevitable, but progress is optional.

With the privilege of leadership comes the responsibility for statesmanship and courage, particularly at times of national challenges. America needs every citizen to speak out and see their collective voices transformed into the winds of change. Only then can their leaders best steer.

It is time for people from all walks of life to ask themselves what we can do for our country, because in our hearts we know our country needs our help. I am ready to help America. Are you?

I was in my office on a recent weekend afternoon working on this book. It was a beautiful spring day and the sun was streaming through the windows. The writing has required reflection, both joyous and painful, and as I looked around the room, I realized that my office holds a lifetime of meaningful possessions, shedding light on my values, philosophy, and life's work.

On the credenza behind my desk are photographs and notes from Matt and Cassie, and the other members of my remarkable family. On my walls are pictures of SEIU members at key events during the years in my union family.

On a shelf is a bumper sticker reminding me in times of uncertainty to ask "WHAT WOULD WELLSTONE DO?" Margaret Mead's weighty words shout out from a card, "Never doubt that a small group of thoughtful committed citizens can change the world. Indeed it's the only thing that ever has."

On my modern, glass-topped desk, placed between myself and visitors, are two items that are always in my line of sight to regularly refresh my memory of the possible. The first is a yellow ceramic rectangular plaque, a motivational gimmick that reads, "IF YOU BELIEVE IT, YOU CAN DO IT."

The second is a figurine holding a balancing bar set on a razor blade; the blade represents "the cutting edge." The figurine sways precariously on the thin-edged blade, but the balance bar keeps the figurine from crashing down. The words written on its base: "THE BEST WAY TO PREDICT THE FUTURE IS TO CREATE IT."

America's future is in the balance, especially Matt's and your children's and grandchildren's. It is time to create the future. It is time for teamwork. Time for a conversation among those committed to rewarding and valuing work. Time to build a country that works 24/7 for everyone.

My hope is that future history books will write about this time and say, *At the dawning of a new century, America's leaders came forward, Americans lifted their voices and became the wind that sailed America to a new future.* I believe the American Dream can continue to shine brightly into the future as a beacon of hope to guide the world in shaping a new civilization.

If not us, who?

If not now, when?

Notes

CHAPTER 1

PAGE

1 **The number of phone calls:** Metropolitan Bureau of Rochedale, UK. http://www.rochdale.gov.uk/Living/EduTrain.asp?URL=ed14-19

1 **84 billion emails:** "Worldwide Email Usage 2005–2009," International Data Corporation, December 2005. (http://www.idc.com/getdoc.jsp?containerId=prUS20033705) and "Email Usage Forecast and Analysis, 2001–2005," International Data Corporation, September, 2001.

2 **The entire world's manufacturing output:** "International Trade Statistics 2004," published by the World Trade Organization. 7/10/2004.

2 **Americans work harder:** "Addicted to Work? Sure, Isn't Everyone?" by Abby Ellin, *The New York Times,* August 17, 2003.

2 **Two-thirds of Americans:** "Bring Back the Forty-hour Work Week — and Let Us Take a Long Vacation," by Joe Robinson, *Los Angeles Times,* January 1, 2006.

2 **Median income:** "Income Picture," Economic Policy Institute, August 31 2005.

2 **Costs of medical care:** "Middle Class Progress?" by Christian Weller, Center for American Progress, October 20, 2005. p. 11.

3 **Average household debt:** "Credit or Cash?" by Christian Weller, Center for American Progress, December 12, 2005. p. 1.

4 **Number of Americans working in retail:** *The Wal-Mart Effect* by Charles Fishman (New York: Penguin Press, 2006).

5 **For five years in a row:** Every Washington Post/ABC News Poll since September of 2001 has shown that over 50% of Americans describe the state of the economy as "not so good" or "poor." See http://www.washingtonpost.com/wp-srv/politics/polls/postpoll110305.htm, question 24.

5 *Parade* **magazine:** "Is the American Dream Still Possible?" by David Wallechinsky, *Parade,* April 23, 2006.

5 **Seven out of ten:** "You Can Build a Fortune by Sweating the Small Stuff," by David Bach, Yahoo Finance, October 24, 2005.

5 **Voters expect their children to be worse off ... Just one out of five ...:** Poll conducted by Lake Research Partners, published Nov 22, 2005.

5 **From 2001 to 2004, productivity increased:** "Living Standards not Keeping Pace with Productivity," Economic Policy Institute, March 1, 2006.

5 **More women will file for bankruptcy:** *The Two-Income Trap,* by Elizabeth Warren and Amelia Warren Tyagi (Cambridge: Basic Books, 2003).

5 **Twenty-five percent of jobs:** "Darn, another HRO Acronym: CWO," by Jay Whitehead, *Human Resources Outsourcing Today,* June 2005.

6 **10.2 jobs from age eighteen to thirty-two:** "Number of Jobs Held, Labor Market Activity, and Earnings Growth among Younger Baby Boomers," Bureau of Labor Statistics, August 25, 2004.

6 **Creative destruction:** *Capitalism, Socialism, and Democracy,* by Joseph Schumpeter (New York: Harper & Brothers, 1950).

6 **If history is a guide:** "Creative Destruction" by Richard Foster and Sarah Kaplan, *The McKinsey Quarterly,* 2001.

7 **Federal Reserve Chairman Greenspan:** Testimony by Alan Greenspan before the Congressional Joint Economic Committee, June 9th, 2005.

7 **From 1947 to 1979:** "New CBO Data Indicate Growth in Long-Term Income Inequality Continues," by Isaac Shapiro and Joel Friedman, Center for Budget and Policy Priorities, January 29, 2006.

7 **If the minimum wage had increased:** "Executive Excess 2005," by Sarah Anderson, John Cavanagh, Scott Klinger and Liz Stanton, Institute for Policy Studies and United for a Fair Economy, August 30, 2005.

8 **Median pay for the CEOs:** "CEO pay soars in 2005 as a select group break the $100 million mark," by Gary Strauss and Barbara Hansen, *USA TODAY,* 4/11/2006.

8 **In a recent column:** "Graduates versus Oligarchs" by Paul Krugman, *The New York Times,* February 27, 2006.

8 **Conservative Economist Ben Stein:** "Executives Gone Wild" by Ben Stein, *The New York Times,* December 18, 2005, and "New Front: Protecting America's Investors" by Ben Stein, *The New York Times,* February 12, 2006.

9 **IBM, famous in years past:** Multiple news stories, including *Newsday;* CNN; Benefitsnews, etc.

9 **Michigan's and Alaska's newly hired employees:** "Pension Intervention," by Anthony Archie and Peter Ferrara, Pacific Research Institute, February 2006.

9 **84 percent of workers:** Data from the Bureau of Labor Statistics on Defined Benefit Pension Plans.

9 **Workers ages twenty-five to forty:** Fidelity Retirement Index, by Fidelity Investments. http://content.members.fidelity.com/Inside_Fidelity/fullStory/0,,5245,00.html.

9 **Two out of ten retirees:** "Senior Income Statistics," from the National Committee to Preserve Social Security and Medicare, http://www.ncpssm.org/socialsecurity/seniorincomestats/

9 **Less than 29 percent of workers:** "Retirement Plan Participation and

Perceptions" by Craig Copeland, Employment Benefits Research Institute Issue Brief no. 286, October 2005.

10 **Five out of ten men:** From the 1998 "National Women's Retirement Survey," by the SunAmerica/Teresa & H. John Heinz III Foundation. http://www.hfp.heinz.org/programs/womensret_02.html

10 **A little over half:** "Will more of us be working forever? The 2006 Retirement Confidence Survey," by the Employee Benefit Research Institute, April 2006.

10 **Negative savings rate:** "Credit or Cash?" by Christian Weller, Center for American Progress, December 12, 2005.

10 **Families continue to file:** *The Two-Income Trap* by Elizabeth Warren and Amelia Warren Tyagi (Cambridge: Basic Books, 2003).

10 **Workers over age sixty-five:** Bureau of Labor Statistics, based on 2006 and 1996 Q1 data.

10 **Only half of baby boomers:** "The Retirement Prospects of Baby Boomers," Congressional Budget Office, March 18, 2004.

10 **Surveys conducted by AARP:** "Many Older Professionals Delay Their Retirement," by Kelly Greene, *The Wall Street Journal*, October 2, 2003.

11 **Americans cashed out:** "Middle Class Cash" by Javier Silva, *Demos*, January 10, 2005.

11 **We own less of our homes:** "Middle Class Cash" by Javier Silva, *Demos*, January 10, 2005.

11 **Number one . . . resolution:** *The Two-Income Trap* by Elizabeth Warren and Amelia Warren Tyagi (Cambridge: Basic Books, 2003).

12 **45 Million Americans:** "The Uninsured: A Primer," The Kaiser Family Foundation, January 2006.

12 **Families declaring bankruptcy:** *The Two-Income Trap* by Elizabeth Warren and Amelia Warren Tyagi (Cambridge: Basic Books, 2003).

12 **Half of personal bankruptcy cases:** *The Two-Income Trap* by Elizabeth Warren and Amelia Warren Tyagi (Cambridge: Basic Books, 2003).

12 **The average Fortune 500 company:** "A Delicate Balance" by Joseph McCafferty, *CFO Magazine*, 2005. Also see "How to Control Health Benefit Costs" by Lynn Dorsey Bleil, James Kalamas, and Rayman K. Mathoda, *McKinsey Quarterly*, 2004.

12 **Large urban hospital:** "Jeanette White Is Long Dead But Her Hospital Bill Lives On" by Lucette Lagnado, *The Wall Street Journal*, March 13, 2003.

13 **Survey research:** "Affordable Health Care for All Americans: Reshaping the Debate over Health Care," by Americans for Health Care and the Center for American Progress December 16, 2005.

13 **Price of health care adds:** "Ailing GM looks to scale back generous health benefits" by Julie Appleby and Sharon Silke Carty, USA TODAY, June 23, 2005.

16 **The only group to see their wages grow:** "Why people are so dissatisfied with today's economy" by Lee Price, Economic Policy Institute, January 27, 2006.

16 **10 percent of Americans owned:** "Changes and Undercurrents: Changes in the Distribution of Wealth 1989-2004," by Arthur Kennickell, Federal Reserve Bank, January 30, 2006.

17 **Union workers earned:** "Union Advantage for Benefits grows wider," Labor Research Associates, October 11, 2005. http://www.laborresearch.org/story.php?id=402

17 **Union membership has declined:** Union density statistics from Labor Research Associates, http://www.laborresearch.org/econ_stats.php.

18 *Wall Street Journal* **column:** "A Separate Peace: America is in trouble—and our elites are merely resigned" by Peggy Noonan, *The Wall Street Journal,* October 27, 2005.

19 **Review of the world's research universities:** Statistic cited in "The Hamilton Project: An Economic Strategy to Advance Opportunity, Prosperity, and Growth" by Roger Altman et al., The Brookings Institution, April 2006.

21 **Miami—America's third poorest city:** Statistics from the 2004 American Community Survey by the US Census Bureau.

CHAPTER 2

PAGE

23 **Chinese Communist Party established the ACFTU:** Statistics from the official ACFTU website, http://www.acftu.org.cn/news.htm.

26 **Half of the cement:** "The City that Ate the World" by Deyan Sudjic, *The Guardian Observer,* October 16, 2005.

26 **The amount of square footage:** "China Builds its Dreams, and Some Fear a Bubble" by David Barboza, *The New York Times,* October 18, 2005.

26 **Their new bullet train:** "Faster Than a Speeding Bullet Train" by Edward Cody *The Washington Post,* May 17, 2004.

27 **Shenzhen, a city of 10 million:** "Shenzhen City Urged to Expand Population," *Shenzhen Daily,* May 27, 2005.

27 **Traditional American tactics of "blacklisting":** "China: A Workers' State Helping the Workers?" by Dexter Roberts, *Businessweek,* December 13, 2004.

28 **Incidents of social unrest:** "Social Unrest in China" by Thomas Lum, Congressional Research Service, May 8, 2006.

28 **Over 450 of the Fortune 500:** "Foreign firms' profits total US$200bn," Asia Times, May 24, 2006.

29 **Nearly the size of the city of Chicago:** Geographic data from the Foreign Affairs & Int'l Cooperation Office of Shanghai Pudong New Area Administration and the Chicago Department of Planning and Development.

29 **90 percent of all the scientists:** "Nanotechnology, the S&T Workforce, Energy, and Prosperity," a prediction by Richard E. Smalley, to the

President's Council of Advisors on Science and Technology (PCAST), March 3, 2003. Available at http://cohesion.rice.edu/NaturalSciences/ Smalley/emplibrary/PCAST% 20March%203,%202003.ppt#432,8, Slide8.

29 **Majority of senior positions:** "Firms in China Think Globally, Hire Locally" by Cui Rong, *The Wall Street Journal,* February 27, 2006.

29 **Third-generation technology:** "China Is Set to Spend Billions On Wireless Upgrade," *The Wall Street Journal,* February 27, 2006.

29 **"The World Is Flat":** *The World Is Flat* by Thomas Friedman (New York: Farrar, Straus and Giroux, 2006).

31 **Two hundred multinational corporations:** "Outsourcing is Climbing the Skills Ladder" by Steve Lohr, *The New York Times,* February 16, 2006.

31 **Intel Science Fair Participants:** "Does the Future Belong to China?" by Fareed Zakaria, *Newsweek,* May 9, 2005.

32 **World's first satellite:** Sputnik statistics from the NASA history website, http://history.nasa.gov/sputnik/.

33 **Largest 100 economies:** Comparison of *Fortune Global 500* 2005 data, which uses 2004 annual report information, and 2004 GDP data from The World Bank Group.

33 **Wal-Mart, the world's largest employer:** Originally cited in "Does the Future Belong to China?" by Fareed Zakaria, *Newsweek,* May 9, 2005.

33 **Wal-Mart the thirty-third-largest economy:** Comparison of Wal-Mart's total revenues for fiscal year 2005 with the CIA World Factbook's ranking of countries by GDP for 2005.

CHAPTER 3

PAGE

38 **Ford's basic equation for America:** "The Economics of Henry Ford" by David Leonhardt, *The New York Times,* April 5, 2006.

52 **Studies reveal:** "Undermining the Right to Organize: Employer Behavior During Union Representation Campaigns," by Chirag Mehta and Nik Theodore; Center for Urban Economic Development University of Illinois at Chicago; December 2005. Study commissioned by American Rights at Work.

53 *Hoffman Plastics v. NLRB:* Hoffman Plastic Compounds, Inc. V. NLRB (00-1595) 535 US 137 (2002).

CHAPTER 4

PAGE

55 **From the acme of union representation:** Union density statistics from Labor Research Associates, http://www.laborresearch.org/econ_ stats.php.

68 **Front page of the** *New York Times:* "In Biggest Drive since 1937, Union Gains a Victory" by Steven Greenhouse, *The New York Times,* February 27, 1999.

CHAPTER 5

PAGE

90 **The AFL-CIO's first constitution:** The full text of the AFL-CIO's constitution can be found at http://www.aflcio.org/aboutus/thisistheafl cio/constitution/art03.cfm.

92 **Over twenty-eight proposals submitted:** The complete set of proposals submitted can be found at http://www.workinglife.org/FOL/ proposals. html.

CHAPTER 6

PAGE

101 **Alvin and Heidi Toffler's 1995 book:** *Creating a New Civilization:. The Politics of the Third Wave.,* by Alvin and Heidi Toffler (Atlanta: Turner Publishing, Inc. 1995).

102 **Online retail spending:** "JupiterResearch Forecasts Online Retail Spending Will Reach $144 Billion in 2010, a CAGR of 12% From 2005." Business Wire, Feb. 6, 2006.

102 **Online poker:** "Online Poker-Driving Gambling to New Heights," study by Research and Markets, February 2005. http://www.research andmarkets.com/reportinfo.asp?cat_id=0&report_id=297197&q=poker &p=1.

103 **Online ... dating:** "Love Drives Online Dating Services and Spending," *The Online Reporter,* February 25, 2006.

104 **Megachurches:** "Megachurches Today 2005" by Scott Thumma, Dave Travis & Warren Bird, Hartford Seminary's Hartford Institute for Religion Research (http://hirr.hartsem.edu) and Leadership Network (www.leadnet.org).

109 **Old guilds:** Description taken from the Operative Plasterers' and Cement Masons' International Association of the United States and Canada, http://www.concrete-plaster.com/Aboutus.htm.

109 **5 to 7 percent of the savings:** "US Offshoring: Small Steps to Make it Win-Win" by Diana Farrell, *The Economists' Voice,* March 2006.

109 **AARP describes itself:** From the AARP website, http://www.aarp. org/about_aarp/aarp_overview/a2002-12-18-aarpmission.html.

111 **Union Network International:** See http://www.union-network.org/.

CHAPTER 7

PAGE
117 *What's the Matter with Kansas?*: *What's the Matter with Kansas?* by Thomas Frank (New York: Metropolitan Books, 2004).
118 Unions have no place: "Life Party" by Jay Cheshes, *Boston Magazine*, September 2000.
125 Tomorrow's front-page news: "SEIU Chief Says the Democrats Lack Fresh Ideas" By David S. Broder, *The Washington Post*, Tuesday, July 27, 2004.
130 Jim Hightower: "There's Nothing in the Middle of the Road but Yellow Stripes and Dead Armadillos : A Work of Political Subversion" by Jim Hightower (New York: HarperCollins, 1998).
131 Mario Cuomo once observed: Remarks from a speech to the "New Democratic Coalition" in 1974. See *More Than Words: The Speeches of Mario Cuomo*, by Mario Cuomo (New York: St. Martin's Press, 1994).

CHAPTER 8

PAGE
134 *New York Times* headline: "Looks Like a Recovery, Feels Like a Recession" by Steven Greenhouse, *The New York Times*, September 1, 2003.
134 Productivity increased 68 percent: "The Growing Divide: Inequality and the Roots of Economic Insecurity" by United for a Fair Economy, November 2005.
134 A recent survey of two hundred large companies: "Off to the Races Again, Leaving Many Behind" by Eric Dash, *The New York Times*, April 9, 2006.
135 Harvard economist Benjamin Friedman: *The Moral Consequences of Economic Growth*, by Benjamin M. Friedman (New York: Knopf, 2005).
135 Americans at the 90th percentile: "Where Did the Productivity Growth Go?" by Ian Dew-Becker and Robert Gordon, Brookings Panel on Economic Activity, September 2005.
136 Ray Irani, CEO of Occidental Petroleum: "Pay for Oil Chiefs Spiked Like Prices" by J. Alex Tarquinio, *The New York Times*, April 9, 2006.
136 Real median household income has fallen: "Income Picture," Economic Policy Institute, August 31, 2005.
137 May 2006 meeting of the NDN: Remarks by Robert Shapiro at a meeting of the NDN in Washington, DC, May 3rd, 2006.
137 May 2006 meeting of the NDN: Remarks by Robert Shapiro ...
137 During the past twenty years: "US Finds Anger in South America: Poverty Blamed on American Imperialism" by Mike Ceaser, *Toronto Globe & Mail* August 31, 2002.
138 Those who argue against protectionism: *The Pro-Growth Progressive: An Economic Strategy for Shared Prosperity*, by Gene Sperling (New York: Simon & Schuster, 2005).

139 **American companies lead the world in offshoring:** "The Emerging Global Labor Market" by Diana Farrell et al., McKinsey Global Institute, June 2005.

139 **For the cost of one engineer in the US:** Testimony of Norman Augustine, former Chairman and CEO of Lockheed Martin, before the U.S. House of Representatives Committee on Science, October 20, 2005.

139 **Indian engineers earned an average wage:** "China Tops India in Average Pay," BBC News, November 14, 2005. http://news.bbc.co.uk/2/hi/business/4436692.stm. Salary figure reflects a conversion from British pounds to US dollars using currency conversion from May 2006.

139 **China and India:** "Deep Talent Pool in India? Bah!" by Diana Farrell, BusinessWeek, April 04, 2006.

140 **The results of a recent study:** "Tradable Services: Understanding the Scope and Impact of Services Outsourcing" by J. Bradford Jensen and Lori Kletzer, Institute for International Economics, September 2005.

140 **Jobs that require a college degree:** "Jobs of the Future: No Boom in the Need for College Graduates" by Lawrence Mishel, Economic Policy Institute, July 21, 2004.

140 **Eight of the thirty fastest-growing jobs:** "The 21st Century Workplace: Preparing for Tomorrow's Employment Trends," Testimony delivered Jared Bernstein, on behalf of the Economic Policy Institute to the U.S. Senate Committee on Health, Education, Labor, and Pensions, May 26, 2005.

141 **The real earnings of college graduates:** "Graduates versus Oligarchs" by Paul Krugman, *The New York Times*, February 27, 2006.

141 **More freshmen had fathers who were doctors:** "Class Matters" by Sebastian Mallaby, *The Washington Post*, November 14, 2005.

141 **Three out of one hundred students:** "Left Behind: Unequal Opportunity in Higher Education," The Century Foundation, 2004.

141 **High price of an education:** "The College Cost Crisis: A Congressional Analysis of College Costs and Implications for America's Higher Education System" by Rep. John Boehner and Rep. Howard McKeon, September 2003.

141 **The cost of a four-year private college:** "The College Cost Crisis: A Congressional Analysis of College Costs and Implications for America's Higher Education System" by Rep. John Boehner and Rep. Howard McKeon, September 2003.

142 **Those costs just keep rising:** "Trends in College Pricing," The College Board, 2005.

143 **Analysts at the Center for American Progress:** John Halpin and Christian Weller of the Center for American Progress provided valuable guidance in developing these measures.

144 **Average of 20 weeks:** Bureau of Labor Statistics. http://www.bls.gov/news.release/empsit.t09.htm.

CHAPTER 9

148 **Men who have changed the world:** quote from *The Mind of Napoleon: A Selection from His Written and Spoken Words,* edited by J. C. Herold (New York: Columbia University Press, 1955)

149 **Social commentator Malcom Gladwell:** *The Tipping Point,* by Malcom Gladwell (Boston: Back Bay Books, 2002).

150 **Jackie Robinson:** See the Jackie Robinson Quotations Page by the Baseball Almanac, http://www.baseball-almanac.com/quotes/quojckr.shtml.

151 **Tiananmen Square:** "The Unknown Rebel," by Pico Iyer, *Time,* April 13, 1998.

151 **Thomas Paine wrote in his treatise:** *Common Sense* by Thomas Paine (New York: Bartleby.com, 1999). Published online at http://www.bartleby.com/133/.

152 **"Idea Assassins" emerge:** *The Third Wave* by Alvin Toffler (New York: Bantam Books, 1984).

153 **Federal Insurance Contributions Act:** For more information, see http://www.ssa.gov/mystatement/fica.htm and http://money.cnn.com/pf/101/lessons/18/page3.html.

154 **The portion of the income pie:** "Don't Mess With Success: There's nothing wrong with Social Security that a few changes can't fix," by Merrill Goozner, The American Association for Retired Persons, January 2005.

154 **Eliminating the cap:** "Keep the Social Security Wage Cap: Nearly a Million Jobs Hang in the Balance" by Rea S. Hederman, Jr., Tracy L. Foertsch, and Kirk A. Johnson, The Heritage Foundation, April 22, 2005.

154 **16 of our Gross Domestic Product:** "The Health Care Crisis and What to Do About It" by Paul Krugman, *New York Review of Books,* 3/23/2006.

155 **Institute of Medicine reports:** "No End to Errors: Three Years After a Landmark Report Found Pervasive Medical Mistakes in American Hospitals, Little has Been Done to Reduce Death and Injury" by Sandra G. Boodman, *Washington Post,* December 3, 2002.

156 **Federal Employee Health Benefits Program:** See http://www.opm.gov insure/health/ for more information.

157 **The military's "TRICARE" system:** "2005 TRICARE Stakeholders Report," Department of Defense, 2005. http://www.tricare.mil/stake holders/downloads/stakeholders_2005.pdf.

157 **Medicare is far more efficient:** "Medicare Reform: A Century Foundation Guide to the Issues," The Century Foundation, 2001.

158 **All of the following countries:** Data for OECD countries from "OECD Health Data 2005: Statistics and Indicators for 30 Countries," OECD, Released June 8, 2005. See also "Snapshots of Health Systems: The State of Affairs in 16 Countries in Summer 2004" by Susanne

Grosse-Tebbe and Josep Figuras, European Observatory on Health Systems and Policies, 2004.

158 **Nine out of ten Americans:** "If It's Broke, Fix It," Survey commissioned by Americans for Health Care and the Center for American Progress, Conducted by Gerstein | Agne Strategic Communications, November 2005.

159 **34 million workers today:** Statistic included in remarks delivered by U.S. Secretary of Labor Elaine L. Chao, ASPPA Conference Lunch, Washington, D.C. April 25, 2006. BLS puts total civilian workforce at 150,811,000 in April 2006, so 34 million is just under a quarter—22.6%, to be exact.

159 **Workers do not have any retirement benefit:** "Retirement Plan Participation and Perceptions" by Craig Copeland, Employment Benefits Research Institute Issue Brief no. 286, October 2005.

159 **Study conducted by Fidelity Investments:** "No Surprise: Retirement Savings Well Short of Needs" by Len Boselovic, *Pittsburgh Post-Gazette,* May 12, 2006.

160 **Replace 70 to 85 percent:** Recommendations vary between financial planners, but they tend to fall between 70-85%. The Congressional Budget Office cites 80% as a figure that financial planners often recommend in "Retirement Age and the Need for Saving," CBO, May 12, 2004.

162 **TIAA-CREF:** See http://www.tiaa-cref.org/.

163 **Superannuation:** See http://www.superchoice.gov.au/ and http://www.ato.gov.au/super/ for more information about this program.

163 **Only 48 percent of Americans participate:** "EBRI Notes," Employee Benefits Research Institute, Volume 26, Number 9 (September 2005).

164 **Child Trust Fund:** See http://www.childtrustfund.gov.uk/ and http://news.bbc.co.uk/1/hi/business/2936101.stm for more information about this program.

164 **Rapidly growing in popularity:** "Reverse Mortgages: Stay Home, Make Money" by Sarah Max, MONEY magazine, March 23, 2006.

165 **If you are sixty-five today:** Reverse mortgage calculator provided by the National Reverse Mortgage Lenders Association (http://nrmla.edthosting.com).

165 **42,700 miles of roads:** Statistic from the US Department of Transportation, Federal Highway Administration. (http://www.fhwa.dot.gov/programadmin/interstate.html)

166 **Newsom said when he announced his program:** "San Francisco Mayor Sees Wireless Service as Basic Right," by Eric Auchard, Reuters, October 4, 2005.

166 **According to the Urban Institute:** "Who Graduates? Who Doesn't? A Statistical Portrait of Public High School Graduation, Class of 2001," by Christopher Swanson, The Urban Institute, February 25, 2004.

166 **Congress knew:** From the American Federation of Teachers. http://www.aft.org/topics/nclb/funding.htm.

167 **Committee for Economic Development estimates:** *Preschool for All:*

Investing In a Productive and Just Society by Committee for Economic Development (New York: Committee for Economic Development, 2002).

167 **Study of over six hundred Head Start Graduates:** "Kindergarten Readiness Study: Head Start Success." Interim Report by J. Meier for the Preschool Services Department of San Bernardino County, June 20, 2003.

168 **Students in smaller schools:** speech by Bill Gates at the National Education Summit on High Schools, National Governors Association 2005 annual meeting, February 26, 2005.

168 **Research ... on small schools:** "Small Schools: Research" from the Chicago Public Schools, http://smallschools.cps.k12.il.us/research.html.

169 **Almost all public schools have Internet access:** "Report: Schools wired, but still not Internet savvy" by Alorie Gilbert, CNET News.com, January 7, 2005.

169 **Experts at McKinsey Company:** "World class: Schools on the Net" by Ted Meisel, T. Michael Nevens, Margot Singer, And Karen A. Tate, *The McKinsey Quarterly*, Number 4, 1995.

170 **America's fifty million students:** Statistic from the National School Board Association, http://www.nsba.org/site/page.asp?TRACKID= &CID= 625&DID=9192.

170 **$440 billion annually spent overall on K-12 education:** "Federal Education Funds," National Conference of State Legislators Memorandum by David L. Shreve, January 15, 2004.

170 **Kids with computers at home:** "Surfing the Web Helps Kids Learn," by Colin Allen, *Psychology Today*, July 30, 2003.

172 **An AmeriCorps-type award:** See for example *The AmeriCorps Experiment and the Future of National Service*, by Will Marshall & Marc Porter Magee, eds. Progressive Policy Institute, May 23, 2005.

172 **army's Basic Skills Program:** See http://www.eustis.army.mil/Education_Center/Basic_Skills.htm.

172 **army's High School Completion Program:** See http://education.military.com/money-for-school/army-high-school-completion-program.

172 **army's Continuing Education System:** See https://www.hrc.army.mil/site/education/index.html.

172 **eArmyU:** See https://www.earmyu.com/Login.aspx.

172 **Service members' Opportunity Colleges:** See http://www.soc.aascu.org/.

173 **Quotation from Helen Keller:** http://www.quoteworld.org/ quotes/7536.

175 **Share of the Gross Domestic Income:** "Gross domestic income: profit growth swamps labor income" by L. Josh Bivens, Economic Policy Institute, March 30, 2006.

175 **Corporate tax revenues as a share:** "The Decline of Corporate Income Tax Revenues" by Joel Friedman, Center on Budget and Policy Priorities, October 24, 2003.

175 **The amount those corporations paid:** "Corporate Income Taxes in the Bush Years" by Robert McIntyre and T.D. Coo Nguyen, Citizens for Tax Justice and Institute for Taxation and Economic Policy, September 2004.

175 **Corporations shield money from the IRS:** "A Fair and Simple Tax System for Our Future" in *Progressive Priorities,* Center for American Progress, January 2005.

176 **Eighty-two profitable companies:** "Corporate Income Taxes in the Bush Years" by Robert McIntyre and T.D. Coo Nguyen, Citizens for Tax Justice and Institute for Taxation and Economic Policy, September 2004. http://www.ctj.org/corpfed04an.pdf.

176 **U.S. taxpayers spend billions:** "The Corporate Welfare Budget Bigger Than Ever" by Stephen Slivinski, The Cato Institute, October 10, 2001.

176 **Wal-Marts:** "Shopping for Subsidies: How Wal-Mart Uses Taxpayer Money to Finance its Never-Ending Growth" by Phillip Mattera and Anna Purinton, Good Jobs First, May 2004.

176 **Ending corporate welfare:** "McCain Introduces Corporate Subsidy Reform Commission Act," Press Release from John McCain's office dated April 7, 2002.

176 **Even the low estimates:** "A Fair and Simple Tax System for Our Future" in *Progressive Priorities,* Center for American Progress, January 2005.

177 **Extending the retail sales tax:** "Discussion Brief: Extending the Retail Sales Tax to Services in Washington State," Economic Opportunity Institute, September 2002.

177 **The Bush tax cuts:** "Studies Shed New Light on Effects of Administration's Tax Cuts" by David Kamin and Isaac Shapiro, Center on Budget and Policy Priorities, September 13, 2004.

177 **Raising just the top two tax brackets:** "Revenue Options" in *Budget Options,* Congressional Budget Office, February 2005 (corrected and updated as of March 30, 2006). http://www.cbo.gov/showdoc.cfm?index=6075&sequence=19

178 **What taxpayers should be paying:** "IRS Updates Tax Gap Estimates," IRS, Feb. 14, 2006.

178 **Restoring the dividends:** Analysis of "The Estimated Budget Effects Of The Conference Agreement For H.R. 2 'Jobs And Growth Tax Relief Reconciliation Act Of 2003,'" Joint Committee on Taxation, May 22, 2003. JCX-55-03 (http://www.taxpolicycenter.org/TaxModel/tmdb/Content/PDF/JCX-55-03.pdf) and "Revenue Options" in *Budget Options,* Congressional Budget Office, February 2005 (corrected and updated as of March 30, 2006). http://www.cbo.gov/showdoc.cfm?index=6075&sequence=19.

178 **Replace the estate tax:** "The Estate Tax Is Down, But Not Out" by Leonard Burman and William Gale, Tax Policy Center, December 01, 2001.

178 **Instead of repealing the estate tax:** "Estate Tax Reform Could Raise

Much-Needed Revenue" by Joel Friedman and Ruth Carlitz, Center on Budget and Policy Priorities, March 16, 2005.

178 **A broad-based Value Added Tax:** "Value Added Tax as a New Revenue Resource" by James Bickley, Congressional Research Service, June 14, 2005.

179 **"The 2% Solution":** *The 2% Solution,* by Matthew Miller (Cambridge: Perseus Books Group, 2003).

Acknowledgments

I am grateful to Cassie's beach sisters and Matt's video-game brothers for their ongoing friendship. I thank my loving family, who are my rock-solid supporters. I also thank my union family—my other brothers and sisters—who are my inspiration.

I thank the leaders of SEIU for their courage to confront the future, as well as my SEIU co-workers. They are the most dynamic, fun group of people with whom I could ever imagine sharing a mission. I appreciate every unheralded and unrecognized contributor to SEIU's accomplishments, and my new Change to Win partners for giving me hope.

I thank Don Stillman, who spent many late nights editing, and Eli Staub for his outstanding research and commitment to getting the facts right. I thank John Halpin and Christian Weller from the Center for American Progress for their policy advice. A special word of gratitude to Anna Burger, Gina Glantz, and Steve Rosenthal for their feedback and friendship; to Tom Woodruff, Eliseo Medina, and Mary Kay Henry for their devotion to organizing; and to Doris Butler, Kirk Adams, Judy Scott, Mike Fishman, Gerry Hudson and more friends and colleagues than I could possibly begin to list here for helping to make this possible.

Thank you to Elizabeth Kaplan and Dominick Anfuso, who had faith in me before a word was ever written. I owe enormous gratitude to Emily Loose for her wonderful editing advice.

And finally, I want to thank everyone who encouraged and tolerated me during this book-writing ordeal. I am more grateful than you can imagine.

Special Acknowledgment

I am grateful to my collaborator, Jody Franklin, who is a big part of this book. It could not have been written without her excellent writing and editing skills, or her diligence, determination, and good judgment.

Index

About the Author

Andy Stern is the president of the Service Employees International Union (SEIU), the largest and fastest-growing union in North America. In 2005, he led SEIU out of the AFL-CIO to help build a labor federation equipped to handle the growing challenges of today's economy. Stern is a revolutionary thinker who combines unconventional strategies and vision to ensure that America's workers can achieve the American Dream. Stern believes that government, business, and labor must work together as a team in order for America to prosper in the new global economy.

Stern was born in West Orange, New Jersey, in 1950. He earned a B.A. from the University of Pennsylvania and began his career as a social worker and rank-and-file SEIU member in 1973. His Web site for this book is www.ACountryThat Works.com.